PROUT:
The Alternative to Capitalism and Marxism

Ravi Batra

University Press
of America™

Copyright © 1980 by

Ravi Batra
University Press of America, Inc.

4720 Boston Way, Lanham, MD 20801

ISBN: 0-8191-1187-2 (Case)
0-8191-1188-0 (Perfect)

Library of Congress Catalog Card Number: 80-67184

From confusion comes clarity
From obstacles comes victory
From struggles comes progress

To all those unsung people
who spent their lives for a
cosmopolitan cause

Preface

There is a widespread feeling in America and the rest of the world that humanity's problems are increasingly getting out of hand. Inflation, unemployment, environmental pollution, energy shortage, crime, bureaucratic corruption, excessive greed, pornography, loss of traditional values of honesty and integrity are some of the dilemmas tht afflict almost every nation on our planet today. All existing systems are facing internal fissures and external traumas. Capitalism and Marxism are the two main ideologies currently guiding most societies. The two ideologies, while disparate in many ways, have at least one idea in common—materialism. While capitalism openly exalts the virtues of greed, selfishness and individualism, Marxism regards matter or economic concerns as the foundation of every social phenomenon. While Marxism consideres materialism the prime mover of everything in society, capitalism considers it the ultimate goal of life. The traditional, spiritual values of honesty and selflessness take a back seat with both philosophies. In this respect, there is not much separating the capitalist and Marxist countries, and, for that matter, the so called Third World.

The yawning problems all over the world today display the intellectual bankruptcy of conventional wisdom. There is a need for new ideas. Fresh thought is urgently needed to counter the menace of impending economic and social breakdown. That is where this book coms in. It provides the alternative. It advocates a new socio-economic and political philosophy called Prout. Prout, authored by a leading Indian scholar, P. R. Sarkar, is an acronym for progressive (pro) utilization (u) theory (t). In the pages that follow I show that Sarkar's message is universal and free from dogmatism. It is resilient enough to be capable of solving problems facing all societies.

The book first builds upon the fundamental principles outlined by Sarkar, and then proceeds on their basis to prepare an agenda for socio-economic reform. The recommendations call for radical changes in economic thinking and social structure. They challenge stereotyped views and expose the reader to economic heresy. They question the sacrosanct orthodoxy and dare to introduce a new socio-economic philosophy. But remember that Keynes was once a heretic; so was Adam Smith. The orthodoxy is repeatedly failing today. Let heresy get a chance.

The book proceeds in an unusual way. Rather than move from the analysis to the conclusion, I first present the conclusion and then the analysis. In this spirit, Chapter 1 furnishes a brief outline of economic reforms that flow from Prout. The fundamental principles of Prout and its basic concepts are examined in the next chapter. Chapter 3 deals with Prout's economic system, Chapter 4 with economic reforms in an under-developed country such as India, and Chapter 5 with a detailed analysis of economic reforms applying to a Western economy such as that of the United States. Chapter 6 analyzes Prout's philosophy of history, which lays the basis for the next chapter presenting Prout's political system. Chapter 8 evaluates Prout in relation to extant philosophies of capitalism and Marxism. It also explores such controversial institutions as the Organization of Petroleum Exporting Countries and the multinational corportation, culminating in a brief agenda for world-wide economic reforms. Chapter 9, the final one, presents Sarkar's vision of society.

As usual, I owe my greatest intellectual debt to P. R. Sarkar whose monumental work lies at the heart of my investigation. Others who have contri-buted to my work either through discussions or through their reading of the first draft include Josef Hadar, Prasanta Pattanaik, Thomas Fomby, Arvind Chaudhary, Amar Parai and Kashi Nath Tiwari. Needless to say, I alone am responsible

Preface

for my errors.

I should also express my gratitude to speedy typing by Elaine Brack, Arlene Underwood, Alice McCaulley, Arlene Armbruster, Kathleen Triplett and Sheryl St. Germain. But for their diligence, this book would not have been completed in time.

In writing this book, I have made use of some material from my earlier book, *The Downfall of Capitalism and Communisim: A New Study of History,* and from articles in *The American Economic Review.*

Dallas, Texas   Ravi Batra
May, 1980

Table of Contents

CHAPTER 1

AGENDA FOR ECONOMIC REFORM

This chapter furnishes a brief outline of the economic reforms that stem from my analysis presented in the rest of the book. All these reforms spring from the sound theoretical foundation of what a leading scholar, Prabhat Ranjan Sarkar, calls Prout, which is extensively examined in chapters to follow. Without these changes, the world economies are likely to remain stuck in the quagmire of inflation, unemployment, and poverty amidst plenty. The reforms presented below aim at reducing economic disparities, while eliminating inflation and unemployment.

(i) There should be a link between the minimum wage and the maximum wage. Specifically, the maximum wage for any social activity should be no more than ten times the society's minimum wage.

(ii) Industries producing essential products and raw materials such as oil, coal, electricity, steel, etc., should be nationalized so that private producers cannot blackmail the entire community by withholding supplies. Such industries should be managed by autonomous bodies responsible to the government on the same principles of efficiency and cost minimization as private firms facing tough competition.

(iii) The stocks, bonds and other financial instruments of large corporations producing consumption goods should be distributed among workers, whose elected representatives, with government's help and training, should run the corporations on the principles of cooperatives.

(iv) Private initiative and investment should be limited to small corporations or proprietorships.

(v) There should be ceilings on inherited wealth linked to the economy's minimum wage.

(vi) Except for essential industries mentioned in the first reform, the government's intervention in the economy and society should be at the minimum. It should aim mainly at maintaining competition among economic agents, and promoting interests of the handicapped.

These are some of the major reforms which, as I have said above, flow from Prout, whose concepts and fundamentals are examined in the next chapter. As I show in chapter 5, the Proutist system tackles the major causes of various socio-economic ills, not just their symptoms. For instance, today Big Government is in disrepute and is blamed by many economists for the twin problems of inflation and unemployment. However, is Big Government solely to blame? Is it not the system itself that has produced the need for a giant public sector? Blaming the public sector and trying to reduce its size by means of restrictive fiscal and monetary policies are examples of the scholars' focussing on the symptoms and not on the underlying causes of various dilemmas. As will be seen in subsequent chapters, the economic reforms suggested above strike at the very root of the socio-economic ills. They are directed at where the malady is, not just at what appears on the surface.

Prout is the philosophy underlying a new socio-economic system, and its remedies apply to variegated problems in all types of economies, whether developed or underdeveloped. In the chapters that follow, Proutist principles and policies should be taken to have general application unless specified otherwise.

CHAPTER 2

THE FUNDAMENTALS OF PROUT

Prout is the acronym that Sarkar gives to his economic, social and political philosophy. It derives from what he calls progressive utilization theory, that is, pro taken from progressive, u from utilization, and t from theory, together make up Prout. Prout is a socio-economic theory, but it blends spirituality with productive efficiency and distributive justice. The Marxian egalitarianism and Rawls' sense of justice emerge in it as tenets of morality, something which benefits the individual and society spiritually. Sarkar's views on economics, industry and government are scattered as bits and pieces through his writings. In this and other chapters, I have collected all those bits and pieces into one coherent theme and then appraised them in the light of modern economic theories. The contributions of some of his close students have also been useful in this regard.

Strictly speaking, Prout is not an esoteric theory, but a set of principles guiding the administration of society in various spheres. One might. call it a practical theory, because its emphasis is not on elegant and abstract concepts, but on that which in reality should work and generate maximum benefit for people. It is an idea that rivals with ideological bases of capitalism and communism. However, Sarkar does not characterize it as a reaction to the intellectual bankruptcy of modern-day socio-economic systems, but something which is universal and will be valid for a long time to come. For he regards capitalism and communism as passing phases of social cycles in different civilizations. But the Proutist system is not ephemeral and, having been based on human psychology, spirit and evolution, it should apply to humanity at large and hence to all nations.

3

THE CONCEPT OF PROGRESS

To understand Prout, it is necessary to begin with its concept of progress. In common parlance, the term "progress" is associated with technical and scientific advancement, or anything which enhances the comforts of life. Humanity is said to have made tremendous progress today because life seems to be much more comfortable these days than it was a few centuries ago. People today can travel fast by automobiles and airplanes, whereas only in the last century were they travelling by horsedrawn buggies or bullock-carts. And if we go back to ancient times, people had to travel on foot. Thus progress is commonly understood as an increase in living comforts through scientific inventions, which have eased our lives not only physically but also intellectually. The invention of paper has helped spread the ideas of scholars. People can now engage their minds reading novels and other literature. Thus scientific discoveries may be credited with tremendous advance that humanity has made in the physical and intellectual realm.

All this, to Sarkar, is not progress. To be sure, it has resulted in a great change in the mode of living, but he denies this to be progress because most scientific discoveries have created problems which were nonexistent before. Faster travel today has increased the risk of accident; industrialization has resulted in environmental pollution and cancer and other diseases unheard of in the past; modern medicine quickly cures the malady but generates side-effects requiring further treatment. Even in the intellectual sphere, there is much available to keep the mind occupied, but people today suffer from emotional problems and neuroses that did not afflict them before. Increased comforts in physical and intellectual spheres have been accompanied by deleterious side-effects, and who is to say that progress has really occurred in these realms. Indeed, Sarkar goes as far as saying that progress in the intellectual and physical sense is impossible unless there occurs a spiritual advance at the same time. In other words, the term "progress" in the intellectual and physical spheres is a misnomer [4, pp. 254-62].

Why can progress not occur in the physical and intellectual arenas? Why must any positive development there be associated with a negative movement? The reason lies in the very nature of the universe which exists in a vibrational flow balanced by positive and negative forces.

The idea of universe as a vibrational flow is supported by modern physics which has discarded Newton's concept of absolute space and accepted Einstein's theory of relativity. Einstein's ideas have been advanced further by what is commonly known as the Quantum theory of physics which holds that each and every atom of the universe is at once a wave as well as a particle. The atom is no longer regarded as a solid object by itself. Rather, it has a nucleus in its center around which even smaller particles called electrons move in a continuous flow and at very high velocities. In the atom, there are two opposing forces. The gravity of the nucleus tends to bind the electrons together; this may be called the centripetal force which arises from the positively charged property of the nucleus. But the electrons, which are negatively charged, resist confinement because of what may be called the centrifugal force. If the centripetal force dominates the centrifugal force, the ever-moving electrons appear as atomic particles. Hence the atom is a wave in the sense that its electrons are in constant motion around its nucleus; it is a particle when its electrons rotate in such a way that there is an optimal

5

balance between their resistance to confinement and the attraction of the nucleus.

What holds true with atoms also holds true with molecules which are simply clusters of various atoms bound together through same interplay of the two opposing forces. The interaction between electrons and atomic nuclei is therefore at the heart of all solids, liquids and gases, and, for that matter, of everything else, dead or alive.

Quantum theory thus reveals a basic oneness of the universe. It reveals that the universe cannot be decomposed into small units existing independently of others. Everything is therefore inter-connected. This is how a moving equilibrium has been maintained in the universe since eternity. If there is expansion in one area there must be contraction in another.

It is this interdependence in the cosmos that makes any progress virtually impossible in the physical world. If there occurs a technical change that seemingly makes life easier than before, there must occur a corresponding side-effect adding misery to life.

The introduction of new technology in common parlance means one of two things: it may be a different combination of various factors of production such as machinery and labor to produce the same product at a higher level of factor (usually labor) productivity, or it may be a new product which apparently has more desirable properties than the one it replaces. Regardless of how the technical change is defined, in the ultimate analysis it results in a new combination of electrons crystallyzed into atoms, molecules, and finally into factors of production. If this new combination is positively charged and adds comfort to life, then it being in the physical realm, there

must occur a similar but negatively charged combination making life unpleasant, so that the
moving equilibrium is maintained in the universe.
In view of the interdependent nature of the physical world, it is not surprising that the results
of new technology will be somewhat counterbalanced by a side effect. Therefore, if life
becomes easier in some respects, it will become
harder in some others. No one can laud science
and technology as an unmixed blessing.

Sarkar's claim that progress is virtually
impossible in the physical realm is very strong
indeed. It seems to be incredible, but it has an
internal logic of its own. And today, with
constructive and destructive fruits of science so
visible in all directions, this logic has become
manifestly clear. Can you think of any invention
which while reducing life's boredom has not added
to life's danger at the same time? Repetitive
work is drudgery; when machines do that work, life
seems to be more pleasant than before. If dish-
washers wash our dishes, air conditioners cool our
rooms, clotheswashers clean our laundry, automobiles do our walking and so on, life certainly
appears blissful relative to what our fathers had
to endure in a scienceless world. But then they
did not have to contend with electric shocks,
fatal accidents, air, water, land and noise pollution, noxious automobile fumes, urban congestion,
super-selfishness, high crime, pornography, and so
on.

Indeed, the harm done by an invention varies
directly with its promise of comfort. Coal results in smoke pollution; so does oil. Nuclear
power has none of this; besides it is one vast
reservoir of power. Its promise is many times the
promise of coal, electricity and oil combined.
But then it is many times deadlier than traditional sources of energy. You can move away from
the pollution of oil and coal, but from nuclear

radiation there is no escape. It follows you wherever you go.

Today solar energy holds greater promise than nuclear plants. That is because its dangers are not as yet known. Every scientific device conceals invisible dangers that become apparent much later. When utilizing new technology, we do not expect any trouble from it. This is faulty logic and thinking. Sarkar corrects this thinking by saying that the side effects of every invention are inevitable, because the entire universe is vibrational in nature, and any physical change producing comfort must be counterbalanced by a physical change producing misery.

Nuclear power today appears unacceptably risky. But a recent study by Dr. Herbert Inhaber, an Associate Scientific Adviser to Canada's Atomic Energy Control Board, concludes that solar power may be even riskier than atomic power [5]. Those who see solar power as a panacea for society's energy problems may be disappointed by this, but in view of Sarkar's concept of progress, the solar risk is perfectly understandable.

Does it mean that science should be discarded? Not at all. With all our overwhelming problems concerning energy, population and pollution, our relapse to pre-science days is unthinkable. All it means is that we have to be more cautious about inventions. Before translating any new invention into industrial technology, its side effects should be thoroughly studied, and investments should be simultaneously made in controlling its emissions. More will be said about this in the next chapter.

While the concept of progress in the material sphere is at best dubious, things are no better in the intellectual sphere. The world seems to have greatly advanced in the realm of intellect. There

8

are more scholars today than ever before. People with M.A.'s and Ph.D.'s abound in many nations, and many more are habituated to reading and writing. But has all this occurred without a cost?

People in ancient times were perhaps intellectually backward, but they did not suffer from emotional stress and neuroses. One who reads less is also less prone to mental disturbances, whereas an intellectual is highly vulnerable in this regard. He creates unnecessary problems in his own web of imagination, and often experiences sleepless nights. Hence in the intellectual sphere also progress is unlikely, if not impossible, because the feeling of increased pleasure is likely to be balanced by one of increased pain.

The barometer of progress in the ultimate analysis must be mental pleasure which is really nothing but a mental vibration expressed through the relaxation of nerves; that is, pleasure is nothing but a mental experience emitted by relaxed nerves. On the other hand, pain is just an opposite experience. When the nerves are under tension, the vibration generated in the mind is called pain. In evaluating the impact of science, people usually focus on the conveniences it has provided, while ignoring the nervous tension it has created in our lives. The fact that progress is not likely in the material sphere only means that any scientific change increases both pleasure and pain.

The same holds true with the intellectual activity as well. In most states, mind experiences either pleasure or pain. There may be cases of either mental repression or of mental denial of discomforting things, but such mental states do not last long. Generally, mind is either happy or unhappy. Now the intellectual activity no doubt increases the feeling of pleasure. A person who has won an argument over another is usually very happy and sometimes delirious with joy. But after a while, he will experience a corresponding amount of pain from some other activity of his mind. The reason is that the human mind has a certain mass and volume. Purely intellectual study and analysis fail to enhance this mass; all they do is to increase the activity and play of ideas within a given intellectual arena. With a greater number of thoughts criss-crossing a given mental area, the result inevitably is an increased turbulence and clash in the mind. Hence occur the mental breakdowns; hence the neuroses; hence the growing need for psychiatrists arising in intellectually developed societies.

Is then progress possible at all? The answer is yes. Human existence has three aspects—physical, mental, and spiritual. While the first two aspects are not amenable to progress, the third is. Increased happiness in that sphere is not neutralized by increased misery.

What is spiritual activity? That action which enables the mind to move closer to its own nucleus constitutes a spiritual activity. We have earlier seen that everything in this universe is supported by a nucleus. But the concept of nucleus cannot be limited to matter alone. The nucleus is essential for the stability of every object, every phenomenon, known or unknown. The human mind, then, also has a nucleus, a central idea around which its other ideas revolve.

Now mind may be simply defined as a bundle of thoughts, which are nothing but various sound vibrations pulsating in the brain. The whole universe is vibrational in nature; so is mind.

What is at the center of all the thought vibrations active in the brain? The sense of pure "I." Every action is preceded by a thought. At the heart of all thoughts is this pure I. In all the thoughts such as "I go," "I sleep," "I am eating," etc., the central idea is the idea of pure I, which is nothing but the sense of existence. Hence the sense of existence is the nucleus of all mental action.

The sense of existence, the nucleus of mind, is purely a witnessing entity. In other words, the nucleus of mind is that entity which supports the mental action by its witnessship of that action. For instance, when a person is engaged in a dream during sleep, some other entity must be watching the fact that the person is dreaming. It is because of his nucleus that the person next day remembers his dream.

The nucleus of the mind must be an infinite entity. The mind is not even capable of conceiving the dimensions of pure I, for each and every thought draws support from the witnessing nucleus. Thus, no matter how vast is the measuring rod conceived by a person, the pure I feeling remains outside the scope of mind. The sense of existence precedes every thought. Hence, the feeling of existence is an infinite entity in the sense that its dimensions can be neither measured nor defined. That is why the pure I feeling pervades each and every human mind: it is omnipresent.

The effort of the mind to come in contact with its nucleus is what we call spiritual activity. Hence, the goal in the spiritual arena is not finite, but infinite. There the resulting feeling of pleasure is not accompanied by pain, or happiness by misery. This, then, is true progress. In the spiritual experience, there is no negative movement; every effort there is a forward march unaccompanied by any deleterious side effect.

11

Spiritual activities include meditation and selfless living. If mind is to move towards its nucleus, then it must contemplate on its sense of existence. It must move inwards, towards its own center. And in the process, it will become selfless. For when the mind moves outwards, that is to say when it runs mainly after materialistic objects, then it moves away from its nucleus, and in the process becomes greedy and self-centered. Hence, meditation, which is the same thing as contemplation of the pure I, by taking the mind away from material objects, makes it selfless. The converse is also true. Selfless living adds to the meditative quality of the mind. Hence spiritual activities include meditation on the nucleus along with selfless living: selflessness is the essence of all spirituality.

Why should the spiritual activity lead to any pleasure? It has been explained before that pleasure is a mental vibration emitted by relaxed nerves. Since with spirituality mind's goal is the infinite entity, the spiritual life generates an expansion in the volume as well as the mass of mind. A given interplay of thoughts and ideas occurs in a much bigger receptacle. As a result the mental conflict declines and the nerves get relaxation. The person becomes broad-minded. He seeks to serve others, to share in their pains. A community which respects the selfless beings and attempts to emulate them also then experiences increased happiness without suffering corresponding pain. That is when true progress occurs in the entire society. The degree of selflessness, therefore, is the true gauge of society's progress, not its material development, nor its intellectual attainments.

While real progress is unlikely in the material and mental sphere, Sarkar does not advocate that scientific and intellectual pursuits should be abandoned. Quite the contrary, he is a champion of science, art, and literature. But he insists that they should be "spiritualized"; that is to say, they should be accompanied by spiritual practices at the same time. For such practices enable us to gain increasing mastery over our bodies and minds. And all detrimental effects of scientific and intellectual developments on the human organism can be thus brought under control.

The introduction of new technology increases the pace of life. More decisions than before have to be made in a relatively short span of time; one has to move fast from place to place in order to cope with the speed of machines. All this adversely affects the nerves, and in turn puts more stress on the brain and the heart. Heart failures and mental agonies are the inevitable by-products of science and technology. Spiritual practices, which calm the nerves, are therefore indispensable if we intend to master science and not be mastered by it.

THE CONCEPT OF RESOURCES

Another concept introduced by Sarkar deals with the notion of resources. Ordinarily, resources are defined to include a society's stock of capital, labor and land, its mineral wealth, its level of education, knowledge, and technology. Sarkar's concept of resources includes these and much more. Here, as with everything else, Sarkar begins with fundamentals. He distinguishes between the resources available to an individual and those available to society. Although such distinction is not apparent at times, it is useful to keep it in mind. Not all individual resources may be available for collective utilization by society.

Let us begin with individual resources, which may be categorized as physical, mental, and spiri-

13

tual. The meaning of physical resource is obvious: it derives from the human body, its health, strength and stamina. The healthier a person is, the greater is his capacity for work as well as enjoyment. The mental resource includes the human mind and intellect. This is what we need to acquire education, skills, or what economists call human capital. Mental resources are subtler than physical resources. Anything conceivable only as an idea is subtle and that which is conceivable as an idea as well as a physical reality may be defined to be crude. It is in this sense that human capital is subtler than physical resources. Our capacity for work and enjoyment also depends on our mental strength, stamina, and intelligence. Specifically, mental resources signify ideas, concepts, languages, literature, art, scientific and technical inventions, and so on.

The third resource possessed by a person is his spiritual resource, one which is slighted by intellectuals today, although this is the most important for individual as well as social welfare. Spiritual resources refer to the knowledge and techniques resulting in the broadening and expansion of mind. They refer to honesty, integrity, and self-sacrifice of which every person is capable. Spiritual resources are the subtlest of the three individual resources, and for this reason are the hardest to acquire. One has to strive to develop them. But the point is that they cannot be excluded from any serious discussion of social welfare, something the modern-day economists and social scientists fail to recognize.

Let us examine the concept of spiritual resource further, for its interpretation is new and needs elaboration. Any individual endowment may be defined as a human resource if it adds to his mental pleasure. For instance, good health and high education are defined by economists as human resources because they add to an individual's productivity and earning capacity and through them to his happiness. A spiritual technique such as meditation and selfless living does the same thing. It may work indirectly through the medium of increased earning capacity, or directly by expanding the volume and mass of mind. In either case, it adds to an individual's happiness. Meditation, for instance, is known to impart concentration to the mind and thus make it more intelligent. Similarly, it tends to calm the nerves, thereby making the individual more productive than before. Selfless and honest living also tend to calm and in addition expand the mind. An expanded mind can better handle the turbulence caused by the ceaseless flow of thought vibrations. It can maintain its cool even under pressure. And not falling apart under pressure is a part of what we call happiness.

A simple analogy will perhaps explain my argument. Suppose you drop a small stone in a jar of water. There will be commotion in water and the jar will be somewhat disturbed. But suppose you drop the same stone in a pond; there still will be some ripples, but they will hardly be noticeable, leaving the pond unscathed. Here the pond and jar may be compared to the human mind, and the stone to external pressures. If the mind is vast, it can withstand the commotions caused by external assaults and retain its cool and happiness. On the other hand, if the mental area is small, even a little shock will cause large ripples in it, leading to misery and tension. Those practices and mental exercises which make the mind vast, thereby adding to its capacity to remain unruffled and happy, are the spiritual resources. Just as without studying and hardwork education and skills cannot be obtained, similarly without meditative exercises and selfless life the spiritual resource remains undeveloped. But the point is that its potential is there in every

15

human being, and a complete theory of social welfare should not disregard it.

Let us now explore the resources available to society. The universe is composed of five rudimental factors, namely the etheral, aerial, luminous, liquid and solid factors. The ethereal factor is simply space, or the void through which sound can pass. The aerial factor consists of all the gases, the luminous factor of light and fire, the liquid factor of water, oils, etc., the solid factor of galaxies, stars, planets, down to our earth. To Sarkar, all these five rudimental factors constitute resources available to society for utilization. He groups them in three generic categories and calls them causal, subtle and crude. For instance, the solid factor is the crude factor, whereas the ethereal is the causal factor in the sense that it is the source of the remaining four rudimental factors. The aerial factor has sprung from the ethereal factor, the luminous from the aerial, the liquid from the luminous, and, finally, the solid from the liquid factor. In this way, the rudimental factors are inter-connected. For instance, if two parts of hydrogen gas are mixed with one part of oxygen, water, the liquid factor, is born.

Modern physics traces the birth of the universe to the aerial factor. Some ten billion years ago, there was a big bang in a giant mass of gases, and light, liquids, and solids later resulted from that massive explosion. But what provided support to the huge mass of gases? None other than the ethereal factor.

In our ordering, we may call the ethereal factor the causal resource and the solid factor the crude resource. The other three factors-- aerial, luminous, and liquid--may be termed the subtle resources available to society. In general, the causal is the source of the subtle, and the subtle is the source of the crude.

In addition to the five rudimental factors, society's resources include those available to individuals. Thus Sarkar's concept of social wealth is much broader than any conceived by scholars to this day.

THE PROGRESSIVE UTILIZATION THEORY

The concepts of progress and resources introduced by Sarkar are central to Prout, which is a normative idea, one that explains how society can achieve maximum social welfare and not what it really is. Sarkar argues that society's utilization of all its resources at any moment of time should be such as to result in progress. Hence the caption: Progressive Utilization Theory, or in short, Prout. But progress to Sarkar occurs only in the spiritual arena. Science and technology are important, but they ought to be utilized in such a way that their harmful emissions are kept under control. Therefore, Sarkar's progress calls for harnessing not only the traditional resources such as land, labor, machinery, minerals, and human capital, but all the rudimental factors along with the artistic and spiritual endowments of individuals and society.

How is this progress to be achieved? Here Sarkar presents five guidelines called the fundamental principles of Prout. Some of these principles pertain to static aspects of society, and some to its dynamic adjustment.

It was during a discourse in 1958 that Sarkar first outlined these principles [2]. Later, for the sake of sharper focus and precision, he slightly modified their wording without altering their essence. In my writing, I have followed the modified version which was compiled in a series of

Sanskrit *sutras* or aphorisms. These *sutras* were translated into English in 1967 [3].

1. **There should be no hoarding of wealth without the permission of society.** In the first principle, Prout gets involved with the concept of private property, which, according to Sarkar, is a misnomer. No one brings any property with him at the time of birth, and no one takes anything with him at the time of death. The world is the joint property of all. Everyone has the right to its enjoyment, but no one is authorized to abuse it. Air and light are regarded as free and hence jointly owned by society. Why should the solids, which essentially are transformed versions of air and light, then not be regarded as jointly owned?

Quantum theory has taught us that the whole universe is one mass of energy. Solids, liquids, gases and light are ultimately the constituents of one and the same mass. If light and air are commonly owned by society, why should the solids or the physical resources such as land, capital, stocks, bonds, not be treated in the same way? Is it not illogical to say that everyone has the same right to enjoy the liquid, aerial and the luminous particles of the universe, but not its solid particles? When everything including the human beings are part of one whole, then who owns this or that? Hence private property is a misnomer. It is an outmoded idea which derives from the Newtonian theory of physics wherein every unit is considered separate from every other unit. It is high time that the ideas of ownership kept pace with discoveries of modern science.

There cannot thus be any natural or fundamental human right to private property, nor to private inheritance. However, society may find it expedient to allow some private accumulation of physical wealth. Hence no individual should be permitted the hoarding of wealth unless society so approves.

18

Many inequities and injustices in the world result from the social sanction of private property. This is true today and was so in the past. It is because of the institution of private property that there is considerable poverty amidst opulence in rich capitalist countries. The same holds with poor underdeveloped nations, and with nations basking in their oil and mineral wealth. The very same idea of property sanctifies national restrictions over the transmission of capital and technology to the hunger-stricken nations. Thus the concept of private property has been for ages at the root of many brutalities that enable some persons and nations to be extravagent while a vast ocean of humanity goes undernourished and even starves to death year after year.

Competing concurrently with the notion of private ownership is that of ownership by the State. This idea is supported vehemently in communist and some democratic countries. If private property is a misnomer, so is the State property. If individuals should not be allowed to hoard physical wealth, so be it with the State or government.

In communist countries, the State, or supposedly the society, owns everything. There is no proprietor, and everyone is a wage-earner. This is another extreme and is as dangerous to human progress as the idea of private property. For the State ownership destroys all incentive to work hard, or to introduce new ideas to cope with a constantly changing world. It may even destroy many other individual liberties. Actually the urge to accumulate is natural in human beings. The future is uncertain and most people like to save something for the rainy day. The suppression of this urge is neither desirable nor possible. The past experience of all communist countries tells us just how difficult it is to deprive everyone of all his property. The great repression that the State in the past unleashed on its property-holders in Russia and China could have been avoided if this natural urge to accumulate had been permitted at least a limited expression.

Prout strikes a compromise between these two extremes. In the interest of incentives and initiative, society may allow persons to accumulate some wealth, but this accumulation cannot be unlimited. Otherwise there will be great income disparities resulting in corruption, poverty, personal envy, high crime and excessive materialism attended by all the concommitant problems. For the wealthy tend to have social influence that hinders the distribution of maximum benefit to the maximum number of people.

2. **There should be maximum utilization and rational distribution of the crude, subtle, and causal resources of the universe.** This principle has two aspects--maximum utilization and rational distribution. Maximum utilization signifies the use of all material and non-material resources available to society at any moment in a way that yields maximum satisfaction to the maximum number of people over the maximum period of time. This implies that all those able to work should be provided with employment opportunities, and that techniques of production should be the most modern or as efficient as possible. There might be conflict between these two goals. If the most efficient production methods are highly capital-intensive, their use could collide against the objective of providing suitable jobs to all able-bodied persons. In such cases, the objective of employment has to take precedence over that of choosing the most efficient technique, or else, while using the most capital-intensive technology, the workers in an industry will be provided more leisure time so that all could find employment.

To a materialist the availability of more leisure may amount to wasting time, but to someone who seeks to maximize mental satisfaction, leisure is most welcome. For then he can allocate some time to spiritual practices which in turn increase his happiness. Hence, there may not be any conflict between the twin goals of maximum employment and efficient but capital-intensive production methods. Still the society has to weigh among various alternatives available for maximum utilization, a question taken up later in the fourth principle of Prout.

While goods are to be produced from most efficient technology, the distribution of income among members of society should be rational. Prout, as stated in the first principle, does not advocate the abolition of private property; nor does it advocate completely equal distribution of income. Instead, it calls for rational distribution, one which furthers and does not conflict with the idea of maximum utilization. Only this kind of distribution can be compatible with the system of material incentives without which people will not give their best in the productive process. Sarkar argues that "diversity is the law of nature, equality will never be." Equality is possible only when the entire matter has been converted in the mass of energy; so complete equality amounts to the cessation of all activity--the death of the universe as we know it. Hence, society should not try for complete equality, because such attempts are doomed to failure. What it can do is to ensure equality of opportunity to all so that no one unjustly gets an advantage over anyone else. In addition, it should provide minimum necessities to all its members, and then try to raise the minimum living standard over time. Rational distribution of income is therefore one where (i) the real wage rate is so determined by society that everyone can afford the necessities like food, clothing, housing, education, and medical care, and (ii) the individual's surplus income, over what remains after everyone's minimum

standard of living has been satisfied, is in proportion to his social contribution. Finally,
those unable to work--the handicapped--are also to
be provided at least their minimum physical requirements, whereas people with special skills and
merits should be allowed to share the surplus
income.

3. **There should be maximum utilization of
the physical, mental, and spiritual potentialities
of the individual and collective organisms.** In
the third principle is established a link between
the individual good and the collective good, between individual interests and the collective
interests. Social welfare depends on individual
welfare and individual welfare on social welfare.
Both have to be stressed at the same time; one can
be neglected only at the peril of the other.
While all persons should be provided with guidance
and opportunities to maximize their physical, mental and spiritual potentialities, society should
also be governed and administered on the basis of
morality and honesty. "One must not forget," says
Sarkar, "that collective good lies in individuali-
ties and individual good lies in collectivity."
[3; p. 54]. Social welfare cannot be maximized if
individual interests are neglected. For this reason, everyone should have the freedom of thought
and expression; everyone should be provided the
minimum physical requirements including leisure,
so that he can devote some time to intellectual
and spiritual pursuits. But individual welfare
also depends on the nature of the government or
the collective body. If the government is corrupt
and dishonest, one cannot expect individuals to be
uncorrupt and honest. Hence, the individual good
lies in the social good, and conversely.

What is the collective body? Prout suggests
that in order to keep the government honest, there
should be another institution to serve the role of
a watchdog over the administration. This ombuds-

man type of institution is Sarkar's collective body which should be composed only of morally and spiritually developed members of society. Only those who are selfless and brave, only those intelligent enough to see through the ruse of self-serving politicians can keep a watch on potential mischief by the government. Hence, if the government is to be kept honest, there should be an incorruptible body of staunch moralists overlooking its actions.

4. **There should be a proper adjustment amongst the crude, subtle, and causal utilizations.** The second principle calls for maximum utilization of the physical, mental, and spiritual potentialities of each individual and society. The fourth principle advocates a proper adjustment in all these utilizations, so that individual and social welfare are maximized not only at any moment of time, but also over time. Humanity needs not only static balance in the use of resources and its faculties, but also a dynamic balance.

The requirement of balance in the use of natural resources suggests that society has to maintain a healthy environment or what economists call ecosphere or the biologists call biosphere. A healthy environment in turn calls for proper use of crude, subtle, and causal resources. For instance, if the use of technology results in atmospheric pollution or poisoning of lakes and seas, it only means that an excessive use has been made of subtle resources deriving from the liquid and the aerial factors. It may also mean a faulty use of human intellect which led to the use of faulty technologies. Hence, society has to maintain a balance in the use of all types of resources if social welfare is to be maximized.

Similarly, each individual is to be encouraged to maintain a balance among physical, mental, and spiritual activities. Neglect or excess of

23

any one of them leads to unhappiness. To get the best out of life, all three have to be pursued simultaneously. Each individual should be first encouraged to attend to his body through a program of physical exercises; second, he should be provided a proper education incorporating not only the essential skills of the time, but the ideas of honesty, personal integrity, and the spirit of helping others. Third, the individual should be encouraged to undertake spiritual practices involving meditation and actually going out of his way to help the needy without compensation. Spirituality is not dogma, because dogma mostly contradicts logic. Spirituality leads to broadmindedness and universalism, dogma to fanaticism and bigotry. Spirituality leads to happiness, dogma to superstitions and misery. Hence each individual is to be encouraged to undertake spiritual practices, which in no way interfere with individual beliefs.

Maximum individual welfare calls for a balance among the physical, mental, and spiritual aspects of life. Similarly, maximum social welfare, as suggested before, calls for a dynamic balance in the utilization of causal, subtle, and crude resources. Society can neglect one at the expense of others only at its own peril. Take, for instance, the objective of maximizing the individual standard of living, or the economy's rate of growth. This goal deals purely with the utilization of crude resources with the help of best possible technology. But it could run into conflict with the proper use of subtle resources if it resulted in smog, or excessive carbon monoxide which among other pollutants have contaminated the biosphere in many industrialized countries. It could also lead to grave health problems. It might also require the maximum allocation of people's time to producing goods and services, so that little time would be left for intellectual and spiritual pursuits. In such conflicts, which

24

are inevitably there, society or the governing body will have to strike a compromise among various uses of natural resources and people's time.

The principle of adjustment also requires that as far as possible employment opportunities suit the employee's temperament. As a rule, persons with many-fold assets should be employed in subtler vocations. An intellectual, for instance, should be employed in an intellectual service even if he possesses enough physical prowess of a soldier. Similarly, a person endowed with spiritual knowledge should be given the duty of instructing others in spirituality; or a warrior-type should be entrusted with the defense or police activities and so on. (For definitions of these terms, see [1].)

Spiritual knowledge is rare. That is why spiritualists are the most useful members of society. They are the ones in whom all three qualities--physical, mental, and spiritual--are well developed. They may not be muscular, but they are intelligent, brave and selfless. Hence society should be governed and administered by spiritually awakened persons.

5. **Utilizations should vary in accordance with changes in time, space, and person, and the utilizations should be of a progressive nature.** The proper use of resources must vary with time, space, and person. Every atom and molecule of this world is different from another. Not only that, everything is undergoing transformations all the time. If there is one constant other than the cosmic entity, it is change. Ideas of yesterday are obsolete today, and today's ideas will be obsolete tomorrow. Something worked in the past; but it may not in the future. Therefore, the methods of resource utilization, the productive techniques, the ideas and theories, the spiritual

practices all have to be adjusted and readjusted over time. They may have to be different from person to person, nation to nation, and, in the future, from planet to planet. Not only should resource utilization vary with the environment, it should also be progressive in nature; that is to say it should also result in a continuous spiritual advance of the individual and society. All new inventions, discoveries and techniques should be utilized with this notion of human progress in mind.

The fifth and final principle of Prout furnishes it the quality of adaptability lacking in all other systems. This is what imparts it a universal character and validity. This is what should make it appealing to all peoples on earth, to all societies, to all nations.

References

1. Batra, R. N., *The Downfall of Capitalism and Communism: A New Study of History*, Macmillan Co., London and Humanities Press, New Jersey, 1978.

2. Sarkar, P. R., *Idea and Ideology*, Calcutta, Ananda Marga Publications, 1959.

3. _____, *Ananda Sutram*, Calcutta, Ananda Marga Publications, 1971.

4. _____, *The Great Universe*, Denver, Ananda Marga Publications, 854 Pearl Street, Denver, Colorado, 1971.

5. Weaver, Suzanne, "The Passionate Risk Debate," *Wall Street Journal*, April 24, 1979.

CHAPTER 3

PROUT'S ECONOMIC SYSTEM

The set of principles described in the previous chapter provides the guidelines to maximize
individual and social welfare not only at any
point of time but also over time. Maximization of
individual and social productivity of all material
and non-material resources at any moment ensures
static efficiency in all three aspects of human
existence--physical, mental and spiritual--whereas
the principle of constant and progressive adjustment in the use of resources aims at dynamic-
efficiency. However, the current world economic
systems are incapable of translating these principles into reality. They lack a proper moral and
intellectual atmosphere in which individual and
social welfare can be maximized. Prout, therefore, proposes its own economic system which will
give effect to its fundamental principles.

The purpose of all wealth, according to Prout,
is to satisfy human wants and needs. Wealth is
needed for consumption, both current and future,
but not for excessive private hoarding or
profiteering. Thus private accumulation and/or
the profit motive should not be the sole basis of
producing goods and services. The sole basis
should be consumption. Hence Prout's is a consumption based economy. Note that while excessive
private hoarding is undesirable because of its
social evils, the social accumulation of wealth is
to be encouraged for further investment as well as
for research in all aspects of human development.

The emphasis on consumption or the satisfaction of human needs is worth noting. Many developed countries are currently enjoying prosperity
unprecedented in their history. Their economies
adequately satisfy the physical needs of most of
their citizens. But they also suffer from unpre-

27

cedented inequities in the distribution of their income and wealth, and as a result they have some minorities which are poor. A need based economy would give priority to fulfilling the needs of such relatively poor people. But the sole motive of production in developed countries is profit, something which is admitted in private but not in public. Investment in goods needed by the poor is risky, for the poor do not have the additional purchasing power. As a result, their needs are not adequately satisfied. People with money keep on making new investments in industries catering to tastes of the middle class or the wealthy, because that is where the profit is. New and new gadgets are produced to satisfy the already satisfied wants, and so poverty coexists with plenty. And if the new gadgetry cannot be easily sold, because the wants of the middle class have already been met from the purchase of some durable goods in the past, the manufacturer wastes millions on advertisement urging the public to scrap the old and buy new, sub-quality but high-fashioned goods. All this is a serious misallocation of crude resources.

Are the rich at fault? Not really, because no one likes to lose money, although but for their greed, the opulent could give away part of their wealth to feed the poor. The real fault is with the economic system which allows some persons to be filthy rich while the minimum needs of others go begging.

The same is true of underdeveloped countries such as India, Indonesia among others where pockets of opulence mock the abject poverty of the masses. Hence it has to be granted that in the interest of maximum social welfare, the allocation of resources ought to be based on human need rather than human greed. How Prout ensures this, I will discuss later.

DISTRIBUTION OF INCOME

In the first principle., Prout advocates that
the minimum physical requirements, such as food,
clothing, housing, education, medicare, should be
guaranteed to all. But mimimum requirements are
not given; they vary with time and place. As
human beings evolve, as their anatomy changes, as
more and more scientific advances occur, the
notion of what is minimum also changes. Hence the
concept of minimum necessities has to be revised
over time. Not only that, with general economic
advance, the minimum standard of living should
also be raised periodically. This will ensure the
spread of economic prosperity to all workers and
not just a few privileged sections.

Minimum necessities should be guaranteed to
all by providing them suitable jobs at money wage
rates that can afford the necessities at market
prices. Actually among necessities, Prout advocates that education, housing and health care
should be provided free to everyone, so that food
and clothing are the. only main needs to be met
from one's wages.

All through history, the class of physical
worker has been the one exploited the most. This
was true in all civilizations in the past and is
true in every country today. The reason is, and
was, that of all the workers, physical laborers
have the least marketable skills. Yet their toil
is indispensable to the survival of society. They
perform jobs considered menial and insulting by
others. They truly need and deserve a helping
hand from the state. The government should fix a
minimum wage rate high enough that the relatively
unskilled workers can satisfy their minimum
requirements. There are minimum wage laws in
all democratic countries. But such minima are too
low to make much dent in the poverty of physical
workers. Prout's minimum wage, however would be

high enough to ensure that everyone meets his basic needs.

Critics of the minimum wage concept contend that it causes unemployment and inflation. I will argue in chapter 5 that such will not be the case in Proutist economy.

After the minimum requirements of all have been satisfied, the surplus national income, if any, should be distributed among people in proportion to their contribution to society. In Prout's terminology, this surplus is called *atiriktam*. The rational distribution of Prout actually furnishes a humanitarian and just way of distributing national income or net national product (NNP) which equals gross national product (GNP) minus depreciation of capital. Let A stand for atiriktam, L for labor force and w for the real wage rate corresponding to the minimum standard of living. Then

$$A = NNP - wL$$

Let TP_j be the total product of the jth individual who contributes to the economy more than the minimum real wage rate. Then Prout's guideline for rational distribution suggests that incentive (I) income of the jth individual should be given by

$$I_j = (NNP - wL) \frac{TP_j}{\sum_{j=1}^{n} TP_j} = A \frac{TP_j}{\sum_{j=1}^{n} TP_j}$$

where n is the number of individuals producing more than w.

A simple example will illustrate this principle of distribution. Consider an economy where labor is the only factor of production. Suppose there are five individuals in the labor force, so that L = 5. Let their annual incomes measured in current dollars equal 100, 200, 300, 1000, 1500. Then NNP = 3100. Suppose that the minimum necessities require a wage rate of 500. Then three persons are subsisting on incomes below the minimum living standard, while two are enjoying exhuberent living standards--a situation not far removed from the present-day reality in most countries where a small minority consumes a disportionately large proportion of income. If the economic system is left to itself then most likely the majority of these five persons will be doomed to their substandard living forever. But Prout would ensure each person at least an income of 500 dollars per year, and the surplus would be distributed between the top two wage-earners in accordance with their productivity. Assuming that incomes of the two rich persons reflect their contributions to society--an assumption not always valid--the surplus income can be determined in this way.

and
$$\text{Here } n = 2, \quad TP_j = 1000 + 1500 = 2500,$$
$$A = 3100 - 2500 = 600$$

The incentive income of the person earning 1000 dollars would be given by 600 x (1000/2500) = 240, whereas the incentive of the other rich person would be 600 x (1500/2500) = 360. Hence prior to social intervention, the income distribution looks like

$$(100, 200, 300, 1000, 1500),$$

but from Prout's formula, it becomes

$$(500, 500, 500, 740, 860)$$

This is an illustration of Prout's distributive justice. As can be clearly seen, this distribution of income is not completely equal, nor is it extremely skewed, as the case would be if the collective body did not intervene in the economy. Hence, Prout's system reduces inequality, but does not destroy the incentive to work hard.

What if the NNP does not meet even the minimum requirements of all individuals.   Many under-developed countries are not fully utililizing their resources.   There the NNP may not be enough to satisfy everyone's minimum necessities as defined by Prout.   In this case, of course, nothing will be left for incentive.   Two objec-tions may then be raised to the principle of rational distribution. First, if all the surplus income of those producing above the minimum requirements is taken away and redistributed among the extremely poor and currently unemployed, then the highly productive persons will be discouraged and reduce their own production. This will then result in a national income loss.   Second, the rational distribution of income may increase current consumption and reduce savings, thereby adversely affecting the rate of growth.   This, one may argue, would have many serious consequences especially in view of constantly rising popula-tion.   It could, in the long run, increase the poverty of everyone including the currently im-poverished people.

Prout certainly does not disregard these arguments.   But it argues that currently resources are not being efficiently utilized anywhere in the world.   Not only are the intellectual poten-tialities being wasted, but the material resources are also being misallocated.   In a country where the rational distribution of income fails to pro-vide minimum requirements to all, any production of luxury goods and services is a misallocation of resources.   In such a case, Prout would completely ban the production of luxury items and utilize their plant and equipment to produce goods needed for current and future necessities.   In other

words, Prout will first correct the misallocation
of resources, increase the production of necessities and introduce its system of rational distribution when it becomes feasible.

MINIMUM AND MAXIMUM WAGE

In examining any system of income distribution, one has to tackle a thorny question. What
is the optimum level of inequality in society?
The question takes it for granted that complete
equality of incomes is neither fair, nor possible.
It also presumes that in the absence of state
intervention, the distribution of income is, and
has been throughout history, extremely inequitous
and exploitative of at least the physical worker.

The question of creative inequality has been
raised and discussed by scholars before but no
practical guideline as yet has been devised.
There have been theoretical solutions, but no
workable devices. My main concern here is not
with theoretically sound judgements, but with matters of practical policy.

Some scholars of equality have suggested that
national income should be so distributed that
marginal utility of income is equal for all
individuals. Given that individual tastes are
different, this rule leads to maximum social
welfare without producing complete equality. It
is this argument that underlies the concept of
progressive income taxation adopted by most
countries. This tax takes away proportionately
more money from the richer than it does from the
poorer. Presumably, the tax revenue is meant to
be spent for those with abysmally low levels of
income.

The problem with equalizing individual marginal utilities is that they cannot be computed.
Nor can we have any approximate idea about their

magnitude. For practical policy, the marginal utility rule is imperfect, if not useless. Similarly, the efficency of progressive taxation of income depends on the honesty of the rich person. The success of the policy, therefore, is at the mercy of the taxpayer. What are the chances of this success? Practically zero! There is a well known saying that nobody becomes rich through honest living. We may not be able to prove its validity in a tax court, but most people know that this is the way of life, especially today. The system of progressive taxation, therefore, rests on the honesty of dishonest people. How many rich persons pay their full share of tax in America or in any other country? Their number could be counted on fingers. Even the political leaders in so many countries are known to have illegally evaded their taxes. Hence merely the progressive taxation of income would not do. We have to have a system free of loopholes.

Even if the government can collect enough revenue from the rich, the problem of its distribution among the poor remains. For this distribution also depends on political leaders and bureaucrats who are corrupt to the core. To them their pockets come first, then their relatives, then their friends, and finally, if at all, the needy. This is the root cause of the failure of many welfare schemes in the United States, India and many other countires. Even if the bureaucrats are not corrupt, their mismanagement has often resulted in colassal waste of funds and in fraud on the part of certain beneficiaries. No! Egalitarianism should not rest on governmental dole, nor on the honesty of the taxpayer and the beneficiary. It should be built into the economic system itself. It should function with minimum of governmental intervention. I will presently argue that Prout's economy will generate such a system.

PROUT'S ECONOMIC SYSTEM

What should be done about income disparities in the short run? Prout's system will one day become a reality, but it may take a long time. No progressive idea can be kept in the leash forever, but it takes time, social conflict and sacrifice before it materializes. What should be done to reduce the yawning income gaps in the meanwhile? Stated otherwise, what wage policy should be followed in the short run, so that Prout's rational distribution is achieved?

At the outset, we should recognize that no amount or variety of taxation short of confiscation will mitigate the income inequalities. Since confiscation of income is neither possible nor desirable today, what else should be done? Why not impose a ceiling on the high wage rates? There are two sides to the problem of inequality, namely the extremely low incomes of 'physical workers, and the exploitative incomes of those possessing high dgrees of economic power.

The topmost executive of General Motors earned more than a million dollars in 1978. He along with some economists would argue that that was his contribution to American society. And they would persist, if reminded, that the United States President only makes two hundred thousand dollars. Presumably, the job of the United Sates President is not as important as the job of the chairman of General Motors. Such are the ironies of capitalism.

At the rate of full time work of 40 hours a week or 2080 hours per year, the General Motors chairman earned more than 4,890 dollars per hour. The minimum wage in 1978 was 2.65 dollars per hour. Thus the maximum wage in the United States was more than 1800 times its minimum wage in 1978. How in the name of humanity can such monstrous inequities be justified? And in arriving at this comparison, we are not counting other millions which the General Motors chairman earned from his ownership of property--stocks, bonds, real estate. His was not an isolated example, either. The Chairmen of Ford Motors, IBM, Exxon, Mobil Oil among some others were in the same boat.

The situation is not much different in a developing economy such as India. There the top executive in the private sector earned a total of 223,350 rupees, or more than 1000 rupees per hour in 1978. While the maximum wage is clear in India, the minimum wage is not, for there is so much unemployment; and then so many farm workers earn no more than a kilogram of coarse grain after toiling for 10 to 12 hours a day. If generously calculated, this wage comes to no more than 1/2 rupee per hour. Hence the maximum wage in India was, and is, at least 2000 times its subsistence wage. How in the heavens can we justify such brutal inequites?

In the world economies today, there is a clear-cut need for concepts of minimum wage and maximum wage. The two should be interrelated to preserve a semblance of social justice. This way income inequities can never exceed the bounds of fairness. Under this policy, if the maximum wage rises, so will the minimum wage, and inequities will never grow out of sight.

How should the minimum and the maximum wage be related? Stated otherwise, how much inequality should society permit? It is easier to raise this question than to answer it. Many scholars today believe in the concept of optimum or "Creative" inequality. But devising a mathematical formula for it is extremely difficult, if not impossible. For consider the formidability of this task. An economist would say that optimum inequality is one that fosters productive efficiency and growth. A sociologist would say that it should be just and moral. A "freedom fighter" would say that it should not involve excessive governmental intervention in economic and social affairs. Others would say that it should not impede risk-taking, saving and incentives. There are just too many considerations here to produce a rigorous optimizing model that generates a formula for optimum inequality. It is just not possible to follow the usual method in economics of maximizing social welfare subject to the constraint of resources, simply because the social welfare function contains countless variables not subject to measurement.

Indeed, an argument such as this plays into the hands of the champions of liberty. Since the concept of complete income equality is an easy target of attack, and since a formula for creative inequality has not so far been devised, the apologists of unlimited private property insist that the economic system should be left to itself. But the question is: do we need a rigourous mathematical formula?

Or can we afford to wait for the day until such a formula arrives? In view of the horrendous income inequities pervading all nations today, the answer is no. All we need is a practical guideline to make a start. And for a practical guideline, let us look not towards economists or sociologists, but to the age-old science of numbers. Let us look towards that primeval idea which is the very essence of Nature's diversity and hence of inequality. When the human mind first molded itself out of animality, some two million years ago, it must have been confronted with the thought of one and the many. When it saw a plant and its many flowers, or a tree and its fruit, it must have felt the need for counting-- for numbers in order to make comparisons. There would have been no need for numbers, if everything were one and the same. Hence the numerical idea is the very essence of inequality, and inequality is the basis of the system of numbers.

What did the human mind devise as early as the prehistoric times?   The concepts of one and two! Then three and four, and so on until ten.   To be sure, it must have taken early humans thousands of years before getting to ten.   Nevertheless, the practice of counting based on a system of one to ten can be traced to antiquity.   At ten, the humans took a pause, as the higher numbers could be made of combinations of the first ten numbers. Such was the case in all civilizations.   This system of counting is called the decimal or denary scale, and obviously this decimal scale has survived the onslaught of time.

The ten-based system of counting has been able to measure all of Nature's limitless diversity or inequality.   Is it not suggestive of practical guidelines for social inequality?   It is indeed, for social inequality ultimately derives from Nature's diversity.   If Nature were the same everywhere, there would have been no inequalities in society, for society is a part of Nature.   The decimal scale suggests that the maximum wage should be no more than ten times and no less than twice the minimum wage.   Here is then a practical rule for income inequality.   Here is then a rule for Proutist system of rational distribution.

Complete equality of wages for all occupations is desirable only when no surplus is left after meeting everyone's minimum requirements.   The ideal income inequality on ethical grounds is one where the maximum wage is no more than twice the level of the minimum wage.   Anything less than this disparity would infringe on our sense of fairness and incentives.   However, the ideal may not be achieved for a long time to come.   The second best solution may then be that the highest and lowest wage differ by a multiplicative factor lying between 2 and 10, with the highest wage associated with the office ultimately responsible for society's stability and well-being.

38

Will the system of income inequality based on the decimal scale maximize social welfare? I am not sure; but it will certainly raise social welfare. For the current economic systems where the maximum wage is more than 2000 times the minimum wage is simply brutal, and cannot be defended on any conceivable grounds.

What is so sacred about the decimal scale? Is it scientific or natural? It must be, for nothing illogical or unnatural could have survived from such ancient times. The Egyptians, the Greeks, the Romans, the Chinese, the Hindus, have all used it for as long as can be remembered. The modern day system of numbers is called the place-value method, which is an eternal contribution of the Hindus to humanity. In this system, the Unit is the base and ten is the top of the scale. The same idea is embodied in the ten-based system of income distribution. Here minimum wage, satisfying everyone's minimum requirements, is the base, and the maximum wage is to be given to that person or group of persons endowed with exceptional ability and skills. To Pythagorous, the father of arithmetic, ten was the most celebrated number. In the same way, the maximum wage should be reserved for those making maximum contribution to society.

As a practical guideline, the decimal scale for income distribution is unimpeachable. It is simple, and not riddled with loopholes. Given the will of the people and governments, it should not be difficult to enforce it. Let us not waste any more time and proceed to implement it. Inequality is perhaps as old as humanity itself. The debate over inequality also has ancient antecedents. The constant intellectual bickering in this regard simply clouds the issue and furnishes the wealthy with subtle arguments to justify the status quo. It is high time that intellectuals demanded action from their governments to make economic disparities less inhuman than before. It is high time that they asked for ceilings on maximum wages, rather than welfare schemes so open to fraud and mismanagement. Whenever feasible, and over time, the gap between the minimum and the maximum wage should be narrowed. This could be done by raising the minimum wage faster than the maximum wage. For instance, if the real per-capita income is expected to grow at the rate of 5% a year, then the minimum real wage could be raised at the rate of 10%. As a result, the maximum real wage will have to rise by less than 5%. But all should be permitted to partake of the rising prosperity, so that no one feels left out of the system.

In the U.S., the minimum wage essential for minimum requirements at current prices is approximately 8,000 dollars per year. It means that the maximum wage should be no more than 80,000 dollars per year. This will take care of (i) disparities in individual needs owing to dependents, eating habits, etc. and (ii) the cost-of-living differences. This concept of maximum wage should apply to all the top jobs in government as well as industry. Similarly, nobody should be paid an annual wage less than 8,000 dollars per year regardless of his vocation. I will come back to this issue in chapter 5.

CEILINGS ON WEALTH

So far I have concentrated on labor income, and given perfunctory treatment to incomes from the ownership of property such as stocks, bonds, land, buildings, patents among others. To complete the discussion of an economy's distributive system, the property incomes should also be examined. Indeed, it is well known that in most countries the inequalities of property ownership dwarf the inequalities of income. Some argue that they are the chief source, if not the only source, of income disparities.

40

In computing the maximum wage, the property incomes should also be included, unless, of course, the property-owner is handicapped and is unable to make a living from his labor. But this introduces a serious practical difficulty. Property ownership differs from person to person. If the same maximum income is to apply to everyone, then the maximum wage will also have to differ from person to person. In view of this, we might as well forget about the concept of income ceiling.

For practical reasons, therefore, there should be one standard maximum wage. At the same time efforts should be made to minimize the inequities of wealth. Ceilings should be placed on property ownership as well. As a rule, except in the case of the handicapped, the income from property should not exceed the minimum wage. It is only fair that those property owners who are reluctant to work should be permitted to enjoy a living standard no better than the minimum. Without work, no one is entitled to live better than those who toil all day but still fail to obtain even the minimum requirements from the economic system. All resources are jointly owned by society and property ownership is neither a natural nor a human right. In most cases, it derives from large inheritances. Our birth in a particular family is beyond our control, but individual and social destiny is indeed under our control. It is imperative that as important a social concept as individual's wealth is not left to the chance occurrence of where one is born.

Yet everyone has the right to live. Hence the income from property ownership alone should be neither zero, nor above the minimum wage.

From practical experience we find that different types of wealth earn different rates of return. The rate of return from the leasing of

land and buildings usually lies between 4% to 5%
of their market value.   In places where such property is very scarce, the return could be higher.
For instance, suppose the value of a house in
Dallas is $200,000.   Then its rent normally varies
between 8,000 to 10,000 dollars per year.   On
cash, stocks and bonds, the return normally varies
from 8 to 15%.   The formula for the ceiling on
wealth can then be obtained by dividing the minimum wage by the prevailing rate of return.   If P
stands for property, w for wage, r for rate of
return, max for maximum and min for minimum, then
the wealth ceiling formula is given as follows:

$$P_{max} = \frac{w_{min}}{r}$$

Suppose

$$w_{min} = 8000 \text{ dollars per year}$$

and

$$r = 4\%$$

Then the ceiling on the value of a house, for
instance equals 8000 x (100/4) or $200,000.

Suppose the long run rate of interest on cash
is 10%.   Here the maximum limit on cash holding
equals 8000 x 10 or 80,000 dollars.   This way
ceilings for the ownership of various types of
wealth can be computed.

If a person owns both tangible property such
as urban land and residence and intangible property such as cash and/or shares, he should be
allowed to own the maximum allowable tangibles
plus half the allowable intangibles.   In the
examples given above, the proper mix of both types
of properties would be 200,000 dollars worth of
residential property and 40,000 dollars in cash.
The reason for this flexibility lies in the fact
that the tangibles and intangibles have different

degrees of liquidity. In times of emergency, meagre cash is much more valuable than an expensive residence, for the latter takes time to sell. This rule may allow the property owner a living equal to one and a half times the minimum standard, but it accords with norms of fairness and practicality.

Of course, the wealth ceilings máy differ from city to city, state to state and country to country. This is because differences in the cost of living, social norms, etc. may result in different values for w_{min} and r. But the philosophy underlying the ceiling on tangible wealth everywhere should be that its income does not exceed the annual minimum wage.

In New York, for instance, where the cost of living is very high, the minimum wage may be 10,000 dollars per year. If the return from residential property is 4%, then the property ceiling equals 250,000 dollars. This way property ceilings can be computed for all areas in the world; and they will have to be administered by local governments.

On practical and humanitarian grounds, some exceptions from the wealth-ceiling rule might be provided. The handicapped, the elderly, the widow, may be exempted from the ceiling on humanitarian grounds. The house that one owns and lives in may be exempted from the ceiling on practical grounds. Here the wealth-ceiling would then be either the house or that given by my formula, whichever has higher value. But no one should be allowed to abuse such exemptions. My essential argument is that once we agree on the concept of the ceilings on wealth, it is not difficult to calculate them.

The administration of wealth-ceilings should be afforded some degree of flexibility. Those who live purely on wealth should be provided suitable jobs before their excess wealth is taken away and distributed among the poor. We may call it the socialization of property. However, any wealth in excess of the amount yielding the maximum wage should be immediately socialized, for no one has the right to enjoy a living standard exceeding the maximum wage while his fellow citizens are struggling below subsistence.

Many more questions raise themselves in connection with my proposals. But if we agree with them, the administrative details can be worked out later.

Given the constraint of crude resources in relation to population, the ideal economy in most countries would be one where every able-bodied person has a suitable employment and some property yielding the equivalent of minimum wage. The best of this equivalent would be a house owned by every family.

With a Proutist economy, egalitariansim, as shown in the next section, is built into the system itself. Apart from setting a need-based minimum wage, the government will not have to set ceilings on maximum wage and self-earned wealth, although inherited wealth will indeed be subject to the ceiling commensurate with the minimum wage. Much of income and wealth inequity arises from large inheritances, and once they are made illegal, then in the absence of loopholes, distributive inequities will disappear.

INDUSTRIAL POLICY

Once the question of the distribution of income has been settled, we have to focus on the production of that income. Quite often the two issues cannot be separated, for income distribution may affect national income and conversely. Many economists today argue that we should not

tinker with distributive arteries of the economic
system, for that would adversely affect its productivity and growth. Their main argument is that
any egalitarian policy aimed at income redistibu-
tion would weaken the work-incentive of the rich
as well as their willingness to take risks.
Investment would suffer and so would the national
income.

These arguments are purely specious. If a
person is very rich, what incentive does he have
to work hard? If he already has millions, a few
thousand more dollars are not going to spark him
into diligence. And consider this. The amount of
money that he wastes on conspicuous consumption or
luxuries alone could produce so many extra jobs
for the unemployed. If he refuses to work under
the program of the maximum wage, then he is being
unfair, for there are many more ready to do his
job for a fraction of his salary.

As regards the willingness to undertake new
ventures, I say that such willingness depends not
on how rich a person is but on his temperament.
If he is venturesome and adventurous, then he is
more likely to invest in bold projects than if he
is wealthy. The great entrepreneurs in American
history had more guts than money. They were not
born rich. An adventurous mind likes to take risk
for its own sake, not just to make money.

In any case, Prout's industrial policy is
designed to make egalitarianism an integral part
of the economic system. The redistribution of
income undertaken by the state will be at the
minimum, as it will have to be done only for the
handicapped, the elderly or those unable to work
for some reason. Everyone will be provided with a
suitable job at wages affording at least the minimum physical requirements prevailing at the time.
And if available resources were plentiful, then
the minimum wage will be set high enough to leave

only a small gap between the lowest and highest incomes.

In most countries, whether capitalist, communist or socialist, economic power is concentrated either in the State or in the hands of a few rich persons. This is a well known fact and does not need substantiation. As a result of such massive concentration of economic power, most people in most countries are being exploited in many ways. In some there is ubiquitous poverty, in others all human rights are openly trampled, and in still others poverty afflicts the minorities. The root cause of all these evils is this concentration of economic power and the materialistic ideology that supports it. Prout favors an industrial system based on decentralization of economic power, one in which much of the decision-making is done either by local governments or by workers themselves. It favors a system of cooperative or labor-managed firms supported by an industrial base provided by the State.

If everyone is to be provided with jobs, then industrialization of the whole world is essential. The populations of India, China and the rest of the world are so high that industrialization is indispensable. Agriculture cannot be slighted, but it alone cannot carry the whole burden. Hence arises the need for an industrial policy.

THE PYRAMIDICAL SYSTEM

Prout's economic system compares well with a pyramid. It divides the economy into five major sectors including public, cooperative, private, education and health, with agriculture treated on the same footing as industries. Education and health could be part of the first three sectors, but they have enough features of their own that they deserve separate treatment. So does agriculture, although it may be treated in the same

46

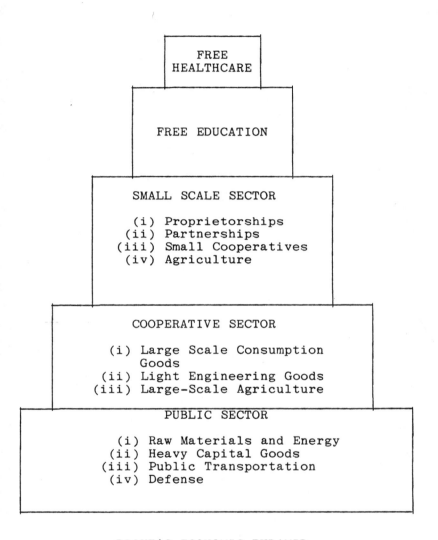

FREE
HEALTHCARE

FREE EDUCATION

SMALL SCALE SECTOR

    (i) Proprietorships
   (ii) Partnerships
  (iii) Small Cooperatives
   (iv) Agriculture

COOPERATIVE SECTOR

   (i) Large Scale Consumption
      Goods
  (ii) Light Engineering Goods
 (iii) Large-Scale Agriculture

PUBLIC SECTOR

   (i) Raw Materials and Energy
  (ii) Heavy Capital Goods
 (iii) Public Transportation
  (iv) Defense

PROUT'S ECONOMIC PYRAMID

way as the large scale cooperatives or small scale
private firms.   The public sector is the base,
producing public goods and intermediate goods, on
which stands the rest of the economic system.
Then comes the cooperative sector, incorporating
large-scale   enterprises   producing   consumer
(including agricultural) goods and services. This
is followed by small-scale industries, based on
individual proprietorship, partnership or small
cooperatives,   producing   final   consumer   goods,
agricultural products, and services.   The final
two steps of the pyramid are free education and
medicare.

Note that the public sector is the base of the
pyramid not because it is necessarily the largest
sector in the economy, but because it should be
the basis of all other sectors.   Similarly, the
second step of the pyramid, the large-scale cooperative firms, should be the basis of the third
step, as small-scale industries should be geared
to large enterprises.   Finally the first three
steps should support the final two.   Let us now
examine these five sectors by turn.

THE PUBLIC SECTOR

In Prout's economy the public sector plays a
very significant role. It is involved in the production of intermediate goods such as raw materials and machinery.   Whether such products are
produced on large or small scale, they are all reserved for the public sector.   Such industries are
the key industries, and they are too important to
be left to the non-public sectors.   The well-being
of the whole society depends upon their adequate
supply, and for this reason the state should be
solely responsible for their production.   This way
no private producer could blackmail the whole society.   Such products as steel, fertilizers, oil
and gas, copper, aluminum, cement, coal, machine
tools,   heavy   engineering   goods,   petro-chemicals

and the like are to be produced exclusively in the public sector. Private investment in such industries should not be allowed. Nor should they be run on the principles of cooperative firms.

They should be run by the immediate state governments. For instance, if a steel plant is located in Chicago, then it should be run by the government of Illinois on the premise that the immediate government best understands the local economic conditions. The public industries are to be run on the basis of no profit, no loss, which means that the price of such goods is equated to the average cost of production. The average cost should be the minimum possible, so that public enterprises obey norms of efficiency. They should use the most efficient techniques, which may or may not be the most capital-intensive. At the same time they should make sure that they do not contaminate the environment. Nor should they generate inhuman working conditions. (I will have more to say on this matter in the section on environmental quality.)

Many people in both the developed and the underdeveloped world today believe that the most capital-intensive techniques are also the most efficient. This is not necessarily true. For one thing, the efficient technique, defined as one resulting in minimum average cost, is that which utilizes a technology commensurate with local costs of labor, machinery and other factors. In a low-wage economy, the most efficient technique may be the labor-intensive one. Secondly, capital-intensive tehcniques generally inflict heavy social costs on the environment in terms of increased pollution. Unless the producer compensates the victims of pollution—which is rarely done—such social costs do not enter into the total-cost calculations. The true average cost, therefore, exceeds the apparent one. Consequently the capital-intensive techniques need not be the most efficient.

Prout calls for a balance in the use of crude, subtle and causal resources as defined in the previous chapter. No single resource should be abused. Hence, social costs of industrialization should be taken into account in industrial decisions.

The average cost calculations should include the costs of labor, a normal return on capital, depreciation of assets, costs of other raw materials, and any costs incurred in eliminating pollution. The price of a public-sector good should be such as to cover all these costs.

The public industries should be run on the same basis as private industries facing tough competition are run in a capitalistic economy. The public-goods sector should not be inefficient, as is the case in all countries today. For this reason, the public sector should be operated by an autonomous body responsible to state governments. The officers of these bodies should be rewarded on the basis of their performance. Their salaries should depend upon whether or not they earn normal rates of return on government's investment. And in industrial operations they should be given a good deal of freedom of decision-making. They should be free to lay off the lazy and incompetent executives and workers. Just because it is a public project does not mean that its employees should be permanently employed regardless of their performance.

In the wage-structure also, hard work and competence should be rewarded, while niggardliness should be punished through demotions and, if necessary, through loss of job. In short, as far as efficiency is concerned, the public industries should be run on the same basis as private industries facing competition.

In addition to the production of intermediate products, the public sector should also be responsible for industries with extremely heavy capital requirements. This is generally true with transportation including railways, airplanes, ships among others. The defense related industries, needless to say, should be in the domain of the public sector.

One can easily appreciate the significance of the role that Prout assigns to the public sector. Key industries, to Sarkar, act as a nucleus that nourishes the rest of the economy. It furnishes the state a powerful tool to direct the allocation of resources into socially desirable areas. For if the country is too poor to afford luxuries, all the government has to do is to deprive them of the necessary raw materials.

Note that Prout's public sector rejects the rigidity and corruption found in the public sectors of communist or socialist countires. Individual initiative within the management of key industries is to be encouraged. Such enterprises are not to be run in the interests of state leaders, as is the case in regimented socialist nations; rather they must be operated in the best interests of all. But they cannot be entrusted to private producers who may take advantage of the rest of society. The oil industry in the U.S. and elsewhere is a pointed example of how private greed can blackmail the whole world.

A few countries today monopolize the production of crude oil which is the life-blood of the world economy. The oil producing countries know this and they keep raising prices. The multinational oil companies also know this and they readily join in this barbaric game, for their profits also rise to dizzying heights. Who suffers? Everyone else! The underdeveloped countries, the brethren of the oil exporting nations, are the

51

most wretched victims. Hence raw materials such as oil, which are the nerve centers of economy, cannot be left to private companies, nor to private nations. (This has implications for a world government, of which I will speak in chapter 7).

THE COOPERATIVE SECTOR OR INDUSTRIAL DEMOCRACY

While transportation, defense and goods used for further production are to remain in the public domain, all final products should be reserved for non-public sectors. Here Prout recommends a democratic system of free enterprise, one in which everyone involved has a stake.

Because of technology, there are some consumption-goods industries which are efficient only under large-scale production; they employ a huge army of workers. Such industries should be owned and operated by workers themselves. Prout, in other words, favors what are usually called cooperatives or labor-managed firms.

It is only under this cooperative system that free enterprise and a free society can truly emerge. When workers themselves, through their elected representatives, are in charge of their destiny, then and then alone can there be real freedom of thought and speech. When a capitalist, or a majority share-holder, is the boss of a company, as is the case in democratic countries, no worker dare speak out against the company's anti-social policies. Who is going to offend the boss for the sake of society? Who is going to bell the cat?

Many private companies in America, Japan, Europe and India have been found to be involved in bribery on international scale. But none of their workers could blow the whistle on them. The Lockheed scandal, the Boeing Company's bribes and countless other cases of corruption constantly point to the fact that capitalist enterprises have to be answerable to those who are the real producers. They must be answerable to their workers. And the best way is to enable the workers to be masters of their own destiny.

The system of monopoly capital prevalent in democratic countries is really a system of corporate serfdom. The word 'serf' usually means a farm-worker attached to a farm. He has no rights of his own; he must work on the farm and receive a subsistence wage. This kind of system prevailed in Russia and the West during 500 years of feudalism [2, chs. 5 and 6].

Whenever there is large-scale unemployment, the industrial worker's status is no different from that of a serf. In India, for instance, this has been true ever since the British took over, and Independence has made no difference. In the West, barring the short period of post-war years, there has been significant unemployment throughout the last three centuries during which industrialization occurred at a rapid pace. There were, of course, periods of boom when workers prospered; but a year or two of their prosperity would be invariably followed by a recession and sometimes depression. With the threat of recessions constantly dangling over their heads, few workers would choose to move from one firm to another. Even though no worker was in theory bound to any single firm, the reality was something else. Hence for a long time in the industrial history of the West, the factory worker could act no differently from the feudal serf. He was no lackey attached to the firm, but his lack of economic power made him a defacto slave.

Today the Western world is passing through stagflation, which combines unemployment with inflation. It faces more uncertainty than any time in the period following the second-world war.

The workers again are afraid of losing their jobs. How can they move from one firm to another? Are they not attached to their companies? Are they treated any better than the feudal serf? Can they dare speak out against their boss if he has done anything wrong? True they are unionized today, and are somewhat better off than the industrial worker of the 19th century. Well! the serfs had also prospered during the heyday of feudalism. A combination of improved technology and urbanization had greatly improved their lot. But they were still called serfs, because their landlords had flourished much more than they had. Today, while the worker is slightly better off than before, the producer simply basks in affluence. There are just too many similarities between farm workers of the feudal age and industrial workers of today. In both cases, property is owned or controlled by the few, and labor for them is performed by the masses. It cannot, therefore, be refuted that capitalism, especially monopoly capitalism, has been for the most part, a system of corporate serfdom.

How can capitalism then be called free enterprise? A stark minority of producers does indeed have all the freedom in the world; but the huge majority of the working class has little say in industries which flourish on its sweat and toil.

Let us look deep in today's factory system. The producer is free to hire and fire a worker. Society allows him to be the owner of huge property, which enables him to control the fate of many persons. When business is good, the producer hires more workers; he pays them a fraction of what he earns. The moment the business slackens, he lays them off. He cares nothing for the starvation of the unemployed. He quickly forgets that the same people had helped him make his millions just a little while ago. They helped him when he needed them the most; he shirks them when they need him the most. And all this because their society has been misguided into believing that ownership of property is a fundamental human right.

The right to live, to speak and think freely, to settle anywhere in the world is our birth right. But the right to property--what ethical and moral sanction does it have? Who brings anything with him at birth other than his body and brains? The universe was here before the first human was born. He did not create it. How can then his progeny own anything?

That no one becomes rich through honest living is a well-known saying which is perhaps more valid today than ever before. The huge estates that some people have inherited in our times could not have been built by their fathers through honest means. Had their fathers not indulged in illegal bootlegging and profiteering, had they not bilked the poor, had they not cheated on their taxes, they could not have assembled vast financial empires. They were able to escape the law through wheeling and dealing. But should we allow their children the fruits of their extortions? (For further details on this point, see the discussion of Robber Barrons in Chapter 6.)

Prout favors the ownership of property not because it is a birth right, but because it accords with human psychology. Everyone likes to save something for the future. If a person accumulates wealth through honest living and hard work, it is only fair that he be allowed to keep what he has assembled; he should also be allowed to pass a part of it to his children. But not huge estates; because by definition they must have been acquired through shoddy means.

For the sake of free enterprise, therefore,

the right to property must be curbed, but not eliminated. The countries where this right has been abolished are fine examples of diabolical tyranny. Russia is the ringleader among such countries. Of course, there what is not permitted to ordinary citizens is reserved for the party leaders.

It is becoming increasingly clear today that concentration of wealth in the hands of a few people, or even nations, is injurious to the health of society. Capitalism is an institution which fosters this concentration, because firstly vast sums of money in terms of profits are distributed among a few shareholders. Secondly, the majority stockholders have enough economic muscle to set their own salaries. The cooperative management of industries by elected representatives of workers will do away with these evils. If factories are owned and managed by laborers, then profits will be distributed among the masses. No longer will a few executives be able to pay themselves whatever they want. There cannot be inequities in the distribution of income in this system. Nor is there any need for the government to introduce welfare schemes to eliminate the nonexistent inequities. Prout is not against profits, but against profiteering. Actually profits are essential if industries are to remain solvent over time, and if investment is to be increased for purposes of growth. But the same profits left in the coffers of monopolists become an engine of massive social exploitation. The cooperative economic system, however, does not permit this. Egalitarianism then becomes part and parcel of the system itself.

Labor-managed firms are not widespread, but they are being tried in some parts of the world. Yugoslavia is a prime example of their success. They can also be found in Britain, Germany, Australia and even the U.S.A. They are, however, the exceptions rather than the rule.

It may be noted that the labor-managed firms are not the same as profit-sharing capitalist firms. With the latter, management and control of the firm still rest with major stockholders, whereas with the former, the workers make all decisions. Labor-managed firms may not be fully owned by the workers; but they do own the majority interest; the rest may be owned by outside shareholders.

The economic literature has lately paid attention to the working of labor-managed firms. Ward [13], Domar [6], Vanek [11] and myself [3] among others have analyzed the decision-making in cooperative enterprises. As usual, among economists, as among intellectuals in general, there is little agreement. The efficiency of labor-managed firms versus capitalistic firms is in dispute. But one thing is clear. The world does not have to change drastically for the labor-managed systems to emerge and operate successfully.

Some suggest that labor-managed enterprises will not be as efficient as their capitalistic counterparts, while others argue to the contrary. Still others argue that the cooperative economic system will be less prone to pressures of inflation and unemployment. While this debate still goes on, some advantages of cooperative enterprises over the capitalist ones are obvious.

First of all, the distribution of income will be more equitable than it is now. Second, workers will work harder when they know that they are entitled to a fair share of profits. This argument derives from ideas supplied by apologists of unlimited private property. They argue that property ownership contributes to our productivity. The same idea applies to the

57

widespread ownership of firms. Third, with more equal distribution of income, crime and other social problems will recede. At times of recession, for example, workers will not be laid off; rather they will accept lower working hours. The system, in short, will be humanized.

There are not many empirical studies available to compare the efficiency of labor-managed economies with the capitalist or socialist economies. But the one done by Balassa and Bertrand [1] conclusively points toward the superiority of the self-managed system. The study found that between 1953 and 1965, the total factor productivity in Yugoslavia grew at a rate of at least 4.5% per year, whereas the comparable figures for the socialist economies of .Bulgaria, Hungry, Poland and Czechoslovakia were all below 2.5%. Only Romania among socialist countries could match the Yugoslav performance. Among the capitalist countries of Greece, Ireland, Norway, the rate of productivity increase in the same period approximated 2.2%. Only Spain had similar performance as Yugoslavia. The study focussed on these countries because they were more or less at the same level of development. And on average the labor-managed Yugoslav economy, with a relatively new and untried system, fared much better than the long established systems of capitalist and socialist countries.

Granted that the large-scale factories producing consumer goods should be run on a cooperative basis, there is a troublesome question that must now be tackled. How can we translate the cooperative economic system into reality?

If some enterprising workers were to get together and with their meager means establish some factories, they will be quickly submerged by the torrent of giant capitalist firms. Even if the state were to give generous loans to teams of

workers willing to start their own firms, they
will have little chance of competing against well-
entrenched monopolies with their operations spread
all over the world. Before such multinational
giants, even sovreign governments shudder. Hear,
for instance, what the U.S. Secretary of Energy,
Dr. James Schlesinger, had to say in the summer of
1979 when the revolution in Iran had abruptly
tightened the supply of oil. At a news
conference, Schlesinger admitted that "using his
power to force allocation of oil supplies to companies willing to refine more gasoline and heating
oil might cause big oil companies to retaliate by
keeping their oil on the high seas or abroad where
it would be beyond the reach of government allocation orders." [5, p. 14A]. The next day Senator
Edward Kennedy was moved to say, "I am appalled
that the Secretary of energy believes that he is
powerless to prevent the multinational oil companies from withholding oil." The U.S. Congress-
man, Richard Ottinger, was more blunt. He said,
"The oil companies are holding us hostage by
refusing to refine more crude oil. Energy
Secretary Schlesinger is clearly content to be
subject to their blackmail."

Schlesinger was just being realistic. No
amount of fulmination from the U.S. lawmakers can
mask the fact that the multinational corporations
all over the world are too powerful to be
controlled by democratic countries. If sovereign
governments cannot stand up to them, what chance
will the infant labor-managed firms have?

The labor-managed firms can become operational
only if the rich controllers of industries are
forced to give away their stocks and bonds to
their workers. This is the only way to rectify
not only the present system but also several
generations of inequities. The controllers have
no right to the industrial wealth because they or
their forefathers must have earned them through

shoddy tactics such as price-gouging or tax evasion. In many countries, the marginal tax rate on high incomes is around 70 per cent. In such a system, how can anyone become a millionaire through intellectual or physical labor without massive resort to loopholes? And the loopholes are available in plenty because the system itself is controlled by the rich. Hence only through shoddy tactics or inheritance can a person become extremely rich. Both of these are unfair means, because the effort involved in self-enrichment is disproportionately small. Therefore given that much of their wealth is undeserved, the stocks and bonds of the current top executives of large cor- porations should be distributed among workers. Other minor shareholders who do not control the management of businesses, i.e., the very small shareholders may be allowed to keep their shares.

The formula for distributing these shares is given by my wealth-ceiling formula presented before. That is to say, no one, not even a worker, is to be intitially allowed to own in- tangible wealth, including cash, stocks and bonds, that exceeds the area's minimum wage divided by the relevant rate of return. Here, again, once the idea is accepted, details can be worked out later.

Let us now come to the question of compensa- tion. It is clear at the outset that if the controllers of industries were to be compensated for the social wealth they say is theirs, society will go bankrupt. I have already argued that no one owns anything from birth. Ownership through inheritance is also suspect if the wealth so transferred is huge because it must have been acquired through dishonesty. Consequently, the controllers of a large firm are not entitled to more than minimal compensation on moral grounds. However, exceptions may be made on humanitarian grounds.

If the shareholder in question is handicapped, old, or cannot work for some reason, then he should be given a suitable pension. He may be permitted an average standard of living, one available from society's average wage. Otherwise, there can be no more than minimal compensation. Of course, the able-bodied industrialists should be provided jobs commensurate with their qualifications. And like any other worker, they are also entitled to minimal wealth.

THE SMALL SCALE SECTOR

The third step of Prout's economic pyramid is the small-scale sector, which is mainly the private-sector, although in some cases goods and services may be produced by small-scale cooperatives. Private initiative fosters economic efficiency and productivity; it should be properly harnessed in the interest of social welfare. But it should not be permitted unbridled expansion, lest it become an instrument of mass exploitation. In recognition of these considerations, Prout encourages private investment and ingenuity, but only in small-scale concerns.

Firms which require small investment and hire very few workers should be left to the private entrepreneurs. Here the organization of the firm may be either individual proprietorship or partnership. And when there are many active partners, the firm is similar to a small cooperative. The definition of what is a small or a large firm should be left to a policy planning body.

The private sector should mainly be engaged in trade and service industries, for they do not require heavy start-up capital or complex technology. Restaurants, grocery stores, tailoring, barber shops, laundries, handicrafts, auto-repairing, book stores and the like constitute this sector. Private practices of physicians and lawyers also come under the small-scale category.

Because of the small size, the private sector will normally operate under conditions of perfect competition. But still the state must make sure that various groups do not combine to follow restrictive trade practices. In the United States and some other countries including Germany and France among others, physicians have formed associations, and effectively controlled the supply of new physicians by limiting the number of medical graduates from universities. As a result, the medical profession enjoys one of the highest living standards in these countries. Lawyers have done the same thing. This is nothing but profiteering. Clearly these practices violate our sense of decency and fairness. Therefore, the state must ensure competition in the private sector. Associations of various groups cannot be outlawed, but they should not be allowed to interfere with educational institutions.

AGRICULTURE

Prout treats agriculture as one of the industries, and assigns it a very important role. Ordinarily, agriculture should have been included within the foregoing analysis of the large scale cooperatives and the small scale sector; but it has enough features of its own, and deserves a separate treatment.

In most developed economies, agriculture is highly mechanized and absorbs between 10 to 30% of the population. In underdeveloped countries such as India this figure is as high as 80%, which is a mark of how far the Indian economy has to go. It is not surprising, therefore, that the labor-productivity in Indian agriculture is among the lowest in the world. Yet, because of favorable climate and bountiful water supplies, India's agricultural potential is next only to that of the United States. Agriculture is also backward in many other underdeveloped countries, and a great deal needs to be done. In its economic set-up, therefore, Prout assigns agriculture a vital role. The following discussion applies mainly to developing economies such as India, where much of the farm-sector utilizes obsolete technologies.

While reducing the proportion of population relying on agriculture, it is not necessary to move people from rural to urban areas. Such movement in the past has caused unprecedented but avoidable problems. Urban congestion and pollution, skyrocketting prices of houses, transportation bottlenecks, etc. in many underdeveloped countries could have all been avoided if small-scale agri-based industires had been established in villages. Such industries should be built around crops available in a specific area. For instance, sugar producing enterprises should be established in an area producing sugar cane, paper industry near a forested area, and so on.

For the efficient production of crops, ceilings on land holding should be fixed at both the minimum and maximum levels, taking into account the area's fertility, availability of water for irrigation and other aspects determining land's productivity. Such ceilings can be obtained from my general formula for wealth limits presented earlier. The maximum farm-income, as with individual income in general, should not exceed the maximum wage. That is to say, in India, those who toil should be allowed to own farm land to the extent that they earn no more than 2,000 rupees per month at current prices. Those who do not toil and must lease their land to farm workers cannot be allowed to own more land than that yielding income in excess of the minimum wage. In other words, an absentee landlord in India should be allowed to own that much land as

63

currently yields a monthly income not exceeding 200 rupees. This way minimum and maximum ceilings on farm land can be computed from my formula.

Those owning the maximum allowable amount of land should be given the option of private or cooperative farming. But those with smaller land holdings should be encouraged to form agricultural cooperatives so that mechanization and large-scale farming can be introduced. The farmers will then not only get a wage for their labor but also a share of profits.

Apart from private and cooperative farming, there should be producer's cooperatives which will be responsible for the sale of crops, procurement of developed seeds, fertilizers, farm machinery, irrigation and other services vital for agricultural production. They would also provide loans at times of need, and purchase crop insurance, so that their members are not vulnerable to unforseen crop failures.

As in the case of industry, the question of compensation arises in the case of agriculture as well. Should the landowners be compensated for any land that they have to give up in order that the ceilings are enforced? The answer again is that there can be no more than minimal compensation. For one thing, the landlords ought to be treated in the same way as other property owners. Secondly, as argued several times before, no body owns any wealth by right. The universe is the joint property of its inhabitants, and if in the interest of maximum social welfare, some wealth has to be taken away from a few people, they are entitled to no more than minimal compensation, for they never owned anything to begin with. Similarly, the government does not own anything either. Therefore, the recipients of land should also not be charged anything. However, the state may encourage the new and old landowners to form

64

cooperatives.

HEALTH AND EDUCATION

Education and health constitute the final two steps of Prout's economic pyramid. A sound economy rests on a system of sound education and health. That is why in Proutist set-up education and medicare are to be provided to everyone free of charge. Private education and health care should be free to exist, but they must compete with their public counterparts.

Public education, for all levels, should be administered by autonomous bodies free of any political or other interference. The quality of education depends on the quality of teachers, on their scholarship, dedication, honesty and integrity. That is why society should respect its teachers and provide them an above-average wage. Teachers on their part must teach their students by setting an example; that is, they should practice what they preach. If the students are to be instructed in honesty and integrity, the teachers will themselves have to manifest such qualities.

Education should emphasize not only theoretical but also practical instruction. In under-developed countries where villages outnumber the cities, the urban-area students should be encouraged to attend annual camps in the rural areas. Students are by nature idealistic, and annual visits to poverty stricken villages will fire up their idealism. They might want to serve the villagers who desperately need help. It will do both villages and students tremendous good. While the rural areas will prosper, the students will become humble and broad-minded.

Free education to all at all levels will open up equal opportunity for material and intellectual advancement to everybody. No one, because of his wealth, will get an advantage over others in this regard. Furthermore, educational opportunities to all will increase the pool of talented technicians, scientists, economists and scholars among others. There will be more scope for new research and inventions. And society will be able to achieve maximum utilization of its intellectual resources.

With education, the health care should also be free. The government should open free clinics and hospitals all over the country. One reason why people accumulate wealth is the uncertainty of future health, especially the health in old age. In many democratic countries, medicare has become so expensive that one critical illness can wipe out a person's life-time savings. No one should be exposed to such risks and worries.

Physicians should be encouraged to work in state health-care institutions, but they should be free to run their own practices. However, medicare is one field where laws of supply and demand do not work properly, if at all. The patient has little bargaining power with his doctor as far as the latter's fees are concerned. Hence the government should regulate these fees; and, of course, they should be so determined that the physicians's income does not exceed the maximum wage. This applies to all specialities in medicine including general practitioners, surgeons, and so on.

ALLOCATION OF RESOURCES

What determines the allocation of resources in Proutist economy? This question, of intrinsic interest in itself, must be raised and answered, if only to see how Prout's economic system compares with modern capitalist and communist economies.

Let us consider capitalism first. Under capitalism the consumer is supposed to be the sovereign, and the producer is supposed to utilize resources in such a way that the consumer needs are satisfied in the most efficient manner. All this, economists contend, happens through the media of market demand and supply. First consumer tastes are reflected in demands for various products. The producers meet these demands by hiring various resources at prices determined in factor markets. Naturally, it is in the interest of profit seeking producers to use technology and factors that minimize the average cost of production. The competition among producers ensures that the consumer needs are satisfied at the lowest possible price approximating the lowest average cost. Thus the consumer is sovereign under capitalism. He determines what the producer will produce. All this occurs through the operation of markets where the consumer presents his demands to which the producer adjusts his supply. In other words, the consumer determines the allocation of resources under captitalism.

The story presented above is the best face of capitalism. Critics contend that such an idealized version exists only in the textbooks of the apologists of capitalism, but not in reality. The reality is not one of competition among many producers, but of market-sharing and at least tacit collusion among a few oligopolistic producers enjoying certain degree of monopoly power. In this set-up, a small number of producers is involved in supplying the needs of an industy. After determining their supplies, the producers act to influence consumer demand through extensive campaigns of advertisement. Therefore, instead of the supplies adjusting to consumer demands, as is supposed to occur in the ideal competitive setting, it is the consumer demands that have to adjust to supplies. Therefore the consumer sovereignty is mostly a myth. It is the producer who under modern-day capitalism mainly determines consumer needs through the glitter of television advertising.

Resource allocation under capitalism is no longer, if ever, determined by the consumer's need, but by private greed. Resources move not towards products reflecting urgent wants but towards those with highest rates of return on investment. This invariably means that investments are attracted by industries with the highest degree of monopoly power. As a result, oligopolistic industries expand at the expense of other sectors. The productive inefficiency of oligopolies is already well known. Hence the most inefficient sectors of the economy expand at the expense of the competitive sectors which usually satisfy the most urgent needs. Thus, it is monopoly power or capitalistic greed that determines the allocation of resources under capitalism today. In a word, the system is inefficient pure and simple.

When we come to the communist economies, the situation is even worse. Under capitalism, the consumer does not have much say in the allocation of resources, but he has some say. The producer does influence the consumer's wants by means of advertisement, but at times despite all his persuasion he may not be able to sell all his product at the desired price. In that case, he has to lower price to attract more buyers. Therefore, even today there is some degree of flexibility in capitalist economies. The famed law of supply and demand still works, although the consumer demands are no longer independent of the actions of suppliers.

Under Marxism, however, there is not even this bit of flexibility. The allocation of resources there is decided by a few political leaders who are interested more in aggrandizement of the state

than in social welfare. The communist state de-
votes a considerable proportion of resources to
military goods (and hence capital goods), so that
consumer needs get slighted by economic planners.
As a result, the output of consumption goods
remains limited, and the consumer demands have to
fully adjust to constrained supplies.

Moreover the Marxist states of Russia and
China, among others, regulate their economies at
all levels. All important economic decisions are
made by a central planning body which is far
removed from local conditions so relevant to efficiency of plants and factories. All factories,
except a few industrial cooperatives involving
handicrafts, are owned by the State. Each factory
is headed by a government manager who is judged by
how well he meets the production target set by the
planner. If, for instance, the manager faces the
target of producing 10,000 shoes a year, then his
promotion depends on whether he meets or exceeds
this target, and not necessarily on the quality of
production. And since the consumer has to make do
with whatever is supplied by the State, the factory manager cares little for craftsmanship. It
should not come as a surprise to find the Soviet
manager producing 20,000 shoes of the same foot.

When even the minor day-to-day economic decisions are made by a central body, then the efficiency of production must suffer, no matter how
carefully the planning is done. Hence the command
economies of communist countries are even more
inefficient than the private capitalist economies.
With both, the economic power is centralized--
under communism in a planning body, under capitalism in a few rich persons. And it is this
centralization which ultimately neglects the
fulfillment of urgent human needs.

Proutist economy is, however, need-oriented.
There the allocation of resources is determined

neither by the profit motive nor by State aggrandizement, but by the urgency of human requirements. Prout has opted for a decentralized
economy in which economic power is concentrated
neither in the State nor in a small aristocracy.
The State is to intervene in only those·markets
which, when left to private producers, are subject
to abuse. Thus, no raw materials vital to the
functioning of society are to be produced in
public sectors.

There are two types of factors of production
needed in the process of production. Inputs such
as land, labor and capital are called primary
factors, whereas raw materials, which are inputs
produced for further production, are usually
classified as non-primary factors. It is the
latter type of factors of which the production
should be reserved for the public sector. The
question of the extent to which the current stock
of primary factors should be allocated to the production of non-primary factors should be determined by a policy planning body in accordance with
the laws of demand and supply. This body will
assess the needs of consumption goods in the
economy, and draw upon availabe resources accor-
dingly. In a developed economy, where markets
function smoothly and efficiently, the planning
body may have a minimal role; but in an underdeveloped economy, its role is indispensable.

It is only logical that necessary goods should
have the first claim on society's scarce
resources. The consumption goods produced in the
cooperative and the private sector should be given
priority in allocating the remaining primary factors and the non-primary factors supplied by the
State. The second priority should be given to
capital goods, which are essential to an adequate
rate of growth. In an underdeveloped economy, all
the remaining primary and non-primary inputs,
after minimum necessities have been produced,

70

ought to be allocated to the production of machines. Nothing should be invested in luxuries, which can be defined by the planning body. In a developed economy, of course, the remaining inputs should be devoted to the production of captial goods as well as luxuries.

Capital goods may be produced in the public or the cooperative sector, depending on the investment requirement and complexity of technology. Light engineering goods may be reserved for the cooperative sector, but heavy machinery such as transformers, cranes, tractors, etc. may be produced in the public sector. Such division among capital goods will also depend upon the country's level of technology and development. But in no case should the public and the non-public sectors overlap.

The role of the private or the small-scale sector should be complementary to the public and the cooperative sectors. Wherever large-scale firms are established, the small-scale firms should also be encouraged to supply spare parts and the repairs. Similarly productive operations within an industry should also be separated. This will ensure further decentralization of economy. Take, for instance, the textile industry, where usually cloth and yarn are produced in the same factory. However, Prout would split the textile operations into two units. Yarn, the raw material for cloth, could be produced in a large-scale firm, but cloth could be produced either by large-scale cooperatives or by smaller economic units. Each weaver could weave cloth with the help of a modern loom in his own home. This is how small-scale industry should complement the large-scale concerns, and conversely.

Prout advocates minimum state intervention in the economy. Except for essential raw materials such as energy, etc., the government's main function should be to ensure competition within industries, so that the laws of demand and supply work freely. Wherever an economic unit has little bargaining power, the government should step in. Otherwise it should keep its hands off the economy. Thus, for instance, patients are at the mercy of doctors; so the physician's fees should be tightly regulated. Similarly, the physical worker, though indispensable to society, always seems to be in abundant supply. He may, therefore, command wages below the society's minimum requirements of food, housing, clothing, education and healthcare. Here again the State should step in and decree a minimum wage. In most other markets, the government need not intervene, because the cooperative economic system is not subject to manipulation by the few. It is a democratic set-up, and the worker's democracy will ensure that no one becomes powerful enough to excercise unusual economic power.

In Prout's decentralized economy, the consumer is sovereign. Economic planning is there, but its role is not to shape consumer preferences and tastes. It is only to see that no one places undue constraints on the supply side. Markets for consumption goods will freely function to meet at least the essential needs of all. Once every worker is guaranteed a wage providing minimum purchasing power at current prices, the cooperative firms and private concerns will produce goods and services to meet the needs of all workers. The public sector will also be geared to these needs, for the government body will produce raw materials only to satisfy the requirements of the non-public sector for non-primary factors. Hence once the government ensures competition among firms within an industry and fixes a proper minimum wage, the allocation of resources at any moment of time will be guided by human needs through the media of demand and supply. This allocation will be efficient in the sense that it will satisfy essential requirements of all, generate an equitable distribution of income wherein profits are distributed among workers, and ensure consumer sovreignty. This is what free enterprise really is. Prout will thus abolish most of the economic evils of the present-day capitalist and Marxist economies.

THE QUALITY OF ENVIRONMENT

Since the 1960s there has been a growing debate in economically developed countries about the quality of life, about the environment in which we live and breathe, about the erosion of subtle values caused by super-materialism. By itself, this is a remarkable development in a world where the gross national product, the sum total of all economic activity, is considered the main index of social happiness, regardless of whether the goods produced cater to urgent needs of each and every citizen. The view that money cannot solve all problems or bring happiness and contentment is slowly emerging in societies which are overwhelmingly materialistic.

What is the cause? The unprecedented environmental pollution and degradation so visible in all directions! The side-effects of science and technology, thus far hidden from the naked eye, have abruptly come to the surface, and with a ferocity that just cannot be ignored. No longer can we ignore the automobile-fumes, the noxious doses of chemicals in urban air, congestion on roads, rivers that spew fire or vomit dead fish, oil slicks that destroy beaches, smog that suffocates our lungs and spirits, airplanes that deafen our ears, nuclear plants and wastes that yield deadly radiation. Nor can we ignore the growing health problems ranging from heart ailments, to respiratory diseases, to deformed babies, to cancer. These are the harmful emissions of our so called progress.

PROUT: THE ALTERNATIVE TO CAPITALISM AND MARXISM

Pollution of the environment is not partial to any country or ideology. Marxist nations are afflicted as much by it as the capitalist nations. Nor have the underdeveloped conuntries been spared, although there the pollution springs from poverty not affluence. Environmental degradation is not a capitalistic disease, but a disease of unbridled materialism.

While there is general agreement today about the gravity of our sickly environment, there is less agreement among scholars about its causes, and its cures. There is a widespread myth that industry is the main culprit; however, modern-day, mechanized agriculture is no less culpable in this regard. Our first task then is to identify major sources of pollution.

First of all there are the obvious contaminants--the factories, which discharge poisonous chemicals in rivers, lakes and streams, and pump millions of tons of pollutants into the air. Secondly, there are the consumers who use acidic detergents that eventually mix in water, and automobiles that poison the air. Finally, there are billions of tons of solid wastes, generated by businesses and consumers alike, for which dumping grounds must be found for storage. Many of these solids find their way into drinking water through the sewage system.

Given that life itself creates pollution, why does society not do anything about it. Various institutions and mores are responsible for it in various countries.

In a capitalist society, the main cause of pollution is the institution of private property and the attending profit motive. Here, the sole concern of businesses, large or small, is with maximum profits. Whether their discharge of chemicals into streams contaminates drinking water or

fouls up the air or impairs public health is none
of their concern. It is not for me to document
the polluting actions by private industries all
over the world. The evidence in this regard is
just overwhelming. And the nuclear plant accident
at the Three Mile Island in the United States is
just the latest example of how far private greed
will go to disregard public well-being. There is
some evidence that the nuclear power plant in
question was unsafe to begin with, but the
electric utility responsible for it is alleged to
have put it into operation to obtain some tax
benefits. And this is not an isolated example,
but a general pattern with captialist firms.

In a competitive capitalist world, the
existence of pollution is an anomaly hard to
explain. The capitalist system is supposed to
solve all its problems by itself through the
working of Adam Smith's famous "invisible hand" of
the market. Apologists of capitalism now admit
that with pollution at least, the market mechanism
does not seem to provide enough safeguards. Their
explanation is this. The producer economizes on
the use of all scarce resources, because he has to
pay a price for them. But water and air are
public property and hence free. Their use and
exploitation cost nothing. Therefore the producer
uses these resources excessively and contaminates
them in the process of production. Economists
describe such social costs that do not enter into
private calculations as externalities or external
diseconomies. They maintain that such diseconomies are relatively unimportant and can be taken
care of without much problem.

So obsessed are the proponents of capitalism
with the concept of private property that, in
order to solve the problem of pollution, they
would divide air and water into private domains as
well. Once air and water are converted into private property, people could buy them or sell them

75

in the market. Then there will be competition between those who wish to use them for pollution and those who wish to use them for living and breathing. The producer will then have to pay for his right to contaminate; it will enter into his cost caluclations, and his very profit motive will induce him to economize on the use of air and water for pollution.

To defenders of capitalism, unrestricted private property is so sacrosanct that they do not care how ridiculous their solutions look. Since the problem arises because some property is public and some private, their solution is to make all resources privately owned. It hardly matters if air and water cannot by nature be divided. And what if the competitive owner of air and water over a certain area became a monopolist one day. Breathing could then become very expensive. Our right to breathe and drink water will then depend on our income.

Another solution, not so ridiculous as the one presented above, is that the government should tax the polluter for pollution damage, or subsidize him for his non-polluting agreement.

In a profit-oriented system, none of these solutions will work. The reason is that non-pollution benefits the entire society; but it does not raise private profit. So why should a business bother about reducing pollution. Moreover, under monopoly capitalism, costs of pollution arising from the tax can be easily passed on to consumers. The consumer will then suffer a double bite: higher prices along with unchanged pollution. Finally, the government bureaucracy is controlled by businesses. Who is then going to enforce the tax?

Let us now analyze the environmental degradation in centrally planned economies of Marxist countries. There is no question of capitalistic greed there, although the State greed remains. Surely the planner, planning for a whole society, must take into account pollution damage in his cost calculations of various projects. But he did not, and does not. For every lake polluted in the United States, you can find another in the U.S.S.R. For every sea-beach blackened by oil-slick in America, you can find one in Russia. For every dose of nuclear radiation in the West, you can find one in the East. The problems of pollution are as staggering in communist countries, as in capitalist nations.

Some of the reasons for pollution in Russia are the same as elsewhere. A Soviet enterprise also pays only for labor, equipment and raw-material costs, but not for social costs arising from contaminated water and air. Non-material resources in Russia have also been treated as free. Production there is not guided by profit motive, but by the. motive of State aggrandizement. Hence the result is the same. Social welfare matters as little there as in capitalist economies. Moreover, State officials in Russia are rewarded mainly by their region's rate of economic growth. The government employees, therefore, favor growth and industrialization at all cost. They do not invest in pollution control which only diverts resources from the production of goods, and could thus lead to lower growth. And as long as it is the welfare of the State rather than of people that guides resource allocation in communist nations, pollution control will remain a dream.

Degradation of the environment spreads across the ideological spectrum. It also afflicts the underdeveloped economies, although for different reasons. The main reason there is poverty. Streets in India are dirty, because there are no resources to clean them. Water is filthy and not fit for drinking, because money to purify it is

77

lacking. In addition to these, India has tried to follow the same path of industrialization as the capitalist and communist economies. The smog over Bombay is as heavy as that over Los Angeles, Tokyo, Moscow and London. At least in the United States today, the automobile fumes are less toxic than before because of the widespread use of the catalytic converter; the same is not the case in semi-industrialized nations of India, Korea, Taiwan, China among others. These countries simply cannot afford to clean up their environment.

So far we have examined some apparent causes of environmental pollution all over the world. What are its basic causes? Here there is less agreement among scholars than what meets the eye.

That the environmental damage is real is no longer debated. What is debated is its severity, whether or not humanity needs to drastically alter its values, its mode of living which everyone cherishes in developed countries and which most want to achieve in underdeveloped countries. The environmental controversy is now polarized into two extreme positions. On the one hand, there are those who argue that the crisis is here; that it is on a scale unprecedented in recorded history, and that we must surgically change materialistic life-styles in developed countries, if an ecological catastrophe is to be averted in the near future. There are others, however, who admit that there is an environmental problem but not a crisis. True, errors of technology have been made in the past, but new technologies can be developed to correct past mistakes. In any case, the human metabolism is resilient enough to adapt to the fast changing milieu, and all we need to do is to divert a small fraction of resources to fight pollution without essentially changing our life-styles.

These are two extreme views. The first emits undiluted pessimism, the second unguarded optimism. Their divergence derives from their perception of what technology can achieve.

The pessimistic view is quite old and owes its origin to Thomas Robert Malthus who alarmed his contemporaries by predicting an imminent disaster arising from the growing pressures of population. Malthus argued that the supply of food grows in arithmetic progression, whereas population multiplies in a much faster geometric progression. Therefore if there is no voluntary or "moral" restraint, then wars, famines and diseases will break out to control the population.

Malthus wrote his essay in 1798. Scientific developments since then have proved him wrong. Population, of course, has grown the way he predicted, but food supply has also kept pace. As a result, there has been no worldwide famine in the 20th century.

It became fashionable with scholars to denounce Malthus and his undue pessimism about the future of humankind. But he has been rehabilitated since the 1960's by writers expressing alarm at the growing pollution and depletion of natural resources. Prominent among the neo-Malthusians are Barry Commoner, Paul Ehrlich and Ezra Mishan. Commoner argues that technologies introduced since the beginning of this century have been ecologically faulty; they have been producing harmful emissions without public recognition. But their cumulative effect has imperilled our life-support system in the ecosphere. As a result we must attend to the damage already done and make use of technologies that keep pollution under control. He contends that the current technology has been an economic success only because it is an ecological failure [4].

79

Ehrlich, in a book coauthored with his wife, argues that the basic cause of environmental degradation is population growth rather than technology. The Ehrlichs do not disregard other problems such as poverty, racial tension, energy, urban blight among others, but they argue that these problems cannot be cured without population control [7].

While Commoner and Ehrlich respectively attribute environmental pollution to faulty technology and population pressures, Mishan blames it on the worldwide mania for economic growth. To him social welfare is uniquely related to neither the GNP nor the expansion of consumer's choice through new gadgetry. In affluent countries the costs of economic growth, he argues, far exceed its beneficial effects. And the relentless pursuit of technology at the expense of other values is nothing but a manifestation of this very mania for growth [8].

While Mishan has questioned the need for continued growth in developed economies, an international group of scholars, identified as the Club of Rome, has questioned our planet's capacity to sustain continued growth. Under the chairmanship of Aurelio Peccei, the Club issued a report entitled *The Limits To Growth*. And the title tells the whole story. The report followed an international approach, examined the five most important variables--population, natural resources, agricultural output, industrial output, and pollution--traced their global growth rates to 1900 and projected them to the year 2100. It concluded that the earth's resources will be seriously depleted early in the next century, causing a drop in population because of a lack of food [8].

By now we have a good idea of the major sources of resource depletion and environmental

pollution. To sum up, the basic causes of pollution, according to scholars, are faulty technologies, exponential growth of world population, and
mania for growth. Not surprisingly, their cures
for the malady aim at controlling these sources of
pollution. Thus, Commoner proposes to replace
ecologically faulty technologies by ecologically
wiser ones; the Ehrlichs call for restraints on
global population; Mishan and the Club of Rome
prescribe a no growth society. Many other par-
ticipants of the environmental debate have called
for a nostalgic return to communion with nature,
to a simpler life devoid of noise and fumes.

PROUT AND THE ENVIRONMENT

Let us now see what Prout has to add to the
environmental debate, which is still raging and is
expected to grow in the future. Our environment
all over the world has become so contaminated
today that any theory dealing with social welfare
must tackle this crisis.

Prout shares many ideas of the environmental
debate, but differs radically from its varied
prescriptions. Sarkar's idea of progress itself
identifies the basic cause of environmental
degradation, and in no uncertain terms. Sarkar is
very emphatic about it. To him, progress is not
likely in the physical realm, with which the
environmental debate has been mainly concerned.
Writing four years before Commoner identified
technical advance as the major source of pollution, Sarkar called for a balance in the use of
material and non-material resources of the world.
His idea of progress carries the following implications for scientific and technological change.

1. In Sarkar's view, every sicentific invention or technological advance that seems to make
life easier emits harmful emissions that make life
harder to some extent. Technical change has been

classified by economists into three categories, namely, capital-using, labor-using or neutral between the use of capital and labor. Technical advance is capital-using if at the old ratio of the wage rate and the rate of interest (assuming it equals the rental of machines) the use of capital or machinery increases relative to that of labor; it is neutral if the capital-labor ratio remains the same and labor-using if the capital-labor ratio falls. Normally it is the capital-using technical change that seems to make life easier, for previously tedious, laborious and repetitive chores can now be performed by machines. But machines use energy, and the production of energy generates pollution. Therefore, increased use of machines leads to increased pollution.

In cases where machine-labor ratio remains unchanged or falls, the technical change by itself does not increase the damage to the environment. But then this kind of technical advance is not usually associated with scientific inventions. It results mainly from improved management or increased division of labor, but not from the invention of new machines. Therefore, we may conclude that only capital-using technical change hurts the environment. The neutral or labor-using change may not.

Wherever industrialization has occurred in the past 200 years, technical change has been mostly capital-using, and no wonder the cumulative effect of the past scientific inventions has now generated unprecedented pollution.

2. Sarkar's definition of progress is forceful and precise. It implies that any scientific invention, including that designed to control pollution, will generate deleterious side-effects or what Mishan calls disamenities. The pollution controlling technologies will generate emissions

of their own. Herein lies the gravity of the environmental problem. It should not be taken lightly, especially in countries where it has already begun to harm health and productive efficiency.

In the United States, under the prodding of the government, factories have installed smokestacks to clean the air. These devices eliminate 99.8 percent of the smoke particulates that would otherwise be released in the air. But the U.S. scientists now report that these smokestacks generate pollution of their own. They release invisible thunderstorms of highly charged electrical particles, which could affect the rainfall in the area.

Those who say that the environmental degradation in industrialized countries can be solved through patchwork taxes affecting the market mechanism underestimate the problem. It would take a monumental national, and eventually an international, effort to undo the cumulative harm of decades of uncontrolled, capital-using technological change that has been unleashed all over the world.

3. Since every capital-using technology must generate harmful emissions, it cannot be left to the private producer, for all he cares to see is its salutory effects on his profits, disregarding its unsalutory and inevitable side-effects on the rest of society. Hence the scientific research should be in the public domain. Private producers may engage in research activity, but no invention should be translated into industrial technology without approval from the government, which will have to determine how far-reaching its side-effects are.

4. The fourth principle of Prout calls for maintaining a balance in the utilization of crude,

subtle and causal resources of the universe. It may be remembered that crude resources include the earth and its solid raw materials; subtle resources include the liquid factor, the aerial factor and the luminous factor; and the causal resource refers to the void of the space through which sound can pass.

Environmental degradation may be defined as an imbalance in the crude, subtle and causal resources resulting from the use of what Commoner calls ecologically faulty technologies. There is no doubt that such an imbalance currently exists in the world. Hence Prout calls for an international effort to clean up the environment.

How can it be done? The environmental cleanliness, as shown above, is not a simple task. Here Prout agrees with Commoner that only new technology can do the job. It is true that new inventions will also generate harmful emissions; but then technologies will have to be devised which not only eliminate previous polluion but also destroy each other's emissions. And such technologies are within the realm of possibility. Diamond cuts diamond: Let technology cut technology.

5. Those who believe that there are limits to growth and call for restraint of population are also mistaken. In Prout's view, the present world population is only a short-run problem arising mainly from income inequities among nations. Population never was, and has never been, a long-run problem. The real problem has been the inadequate use of resources. Malthus could not foresee the tremendous potentialities of technological change which has already occurred since his prophecy of doom. Today's doomsayers are unable to visualize beyond the limited horizon of the spaceship earth. Their concept of resources is limited to our planet even though the historic

journey of many Americans to the moon has demonstrated how myopic their vision is.

According to Prout, the ultimate limits to material resources are provided by the universe, not just by its tiny dot we call earth. If the earth cannot provide living space to all its citizens then humans would migrate to other planets, and build society anew. America was unknown to much of the world until 1492. But that does not mean that it had to remain inaccessible forever. Today our planetary system also seems inaccessible, perhaps devoid of life. But that is the challenge which human spirit will solve in the same way it solved other formidable challenges in the past.

Human intellect created the environmental crisis, human intellect will also solve it. Whether population grows faster or at a slower pace does not matter.

Actually it is impossible to control population on a global scale. One nation or another may be able to restrain its growth, but not the whole world. This is what follows from the law of evolution wherein matter is converted first into unicellar ameba and eventually into multimillion cellar humans. In this evolutionary process, matter must sprout into life. This is the very property of matter. Hence population will keep on growing. It may be checked in the short run through wars, famines and other catastrohpes, and even through family planning. But it cannot remain in the leash over the long run. Hence all efforts to control population are destined to fail, and this is more evident today than ever before.

The growth of population is actually a blessing in disguise. Without large populations to support, the new technologies would have never been operational. Whatever the faults of science, no one can fault it for increasing human mastery over supplies of food which in the past was so vulnerable to vagaries of Nature. Similarly, without large populations to maintain, the human mental horizon would not have been as broad as it is today. With fewer people on earth, societies were first organized into village communes. As population increased, city states were born and then came provinces and finally nations. Thus expanding population has steadily expanded human loyalty from village communes to nations. The human mind and institutions, whatever their contradictions, have slowly become somewhat cosmopolitan. Further increase in population is needed to humanize our nationalistic institutions, which so selfishly want to preserve brutal inequities in the world. For the sake of universalism, population growth is indispensable.

To sum up our discussion, Prout encourages scientific inventions, but they have to be such as to control the harmful emissions of each other. For it must be recognized that every scientific advance will have an unsalutory side-effect. Current population of the world is only a short-run inconvenience. The problem arises from the inefficient use of world-resources. One may object to continued growth in developed economies, but not because there are limits to growth but because it has generated excessive materialism and selfishness in society. As regards underdeveloped countries, high growth rates are needed to solve their problems of survival. This is a matter to which I turn in the next section.

ECONOMIC DEVELOPMENT

Following the second world war, and especially following India's Independence, a number of economists have explored the problems facing a poverty-stricken economy. A huge literature has appeared apparently to solve economic dilemmas facing the poor countries. Such literature, whether theoretical or empirical,is usally classified under the rubric of economic development. Prout offers its own path of development, one which is drastically different from any offered by scholars before.

Most underdeveloped economies display common features. They suffer from shortage of capital and technical know-how, illiteracy, excessive dependence on agriculture, and lack of industrialization. All these features lead to low productivity and chronic unemployment, and that is why the poverty-stricken countries are mainly called labor-surplus economies. Obviously the abolition of poverty calls for the abolition of the causes of poverty, and that means economic planning aimed at the development of agriculture, industry, new technologies and educational facilities. All this requires massive investment which depends on the economy's rate of saving. But in a poor country, savings are low because its national income is low. This is the well-known vicious circle of poverty, whereby a country is poor because it is poor. Hence, the first step in economic development is to raise the economy's rate of saving so that investment can be increased.

There are several ways to increase an economy's saving. The government can force the people to save more through draconian means. This is what Russia, specifically Stalinist Russia, did for a quarter century. Millions of Russians were sent to labor camps where they worked for abysmal wages in government's factories. At the same time, the State charged exorbitant prices for goods it produced, thereby further lowering the worker's consumption. Similarly, agricultural prices were fixed at low levels, so that the agricultural profit, in addition to the profit in its industries, accrued to the State. For a long time, the working conditions in Russia were simply horrible, and millions of people revolted and paid with their lives. This is certainly not a prescription for welfare maximization. No civilized country would like to grind its citizens through such oppression so that the State can prosper.

Other methods recommended by experts and traditionally attempted by the poor economies include increasing savings through taxation or through deficit financing whereby the government simply prints more paper money, purchases resources from the public and utilizes them in new investment projects. Both these methods have been tried before, and they have some merit, although when put to excessive use they can be harmful. For high taxation may be evaded, or it may lead to serious loss of incentives to work. And deficit financing, a form of taxation, can cause serious inflation, hampering the developement effort.

Another source of investment is aid from rich foreign countries. But the rich never donate enough, nor is their donation without strings and motives. It is not surprising, therefore, that whatever meager foreign aid the developing countries have received has done little to abolish their poverty.

Ultimately, each nation has to stand on its own feet, at least until the time a world government comes into being. Savings have to be generated from within an economy, and not under the threat of capital punishment. Prout's answer to the paucity of savings is public educaiton and morality. People have to be persuaded to increase their savings and to reduce wasteful consumption. And even in poor countries, there is a considerable amount of wastage, or conspicuous consumption. People have to be taught that saving is a virtue, as it will ultimately reduce poverty of their children and their fellow beings. People have to be encouraged to sacrifice their present consumption, especially those who can afford it. The virtue of saving has to be presented as a humanitarian idea indispensable for the well-being of all.

It is well known that the power of morality dwarfs the power of authoritarian commands. It also dwarfs capitalistic greed. Will any of us offer to die for millions of dollars? But some of us might, for a cause. Will anyone have his head severed for all the creature comforts? But some of us might for the sake of a selfless idea. Hence, morality transcends brute force and human avarice,and it is this force which Prout seeks to harness to achieve a high rate of saving. The connection between morality and economic development is very real, for consuming less and saving more can be presented before the people as an ideal involving sacrifice for their children.

Will such increased savings cause a decline in social welfare? No! If people are forced to reduce consumption under the threat of death-blows, there is certainly unimaginable misery in society. But when someone willingly makes sacrifices, especially for a cosmopolitan idea such as general economic development, individual welfare actually rises. Mind feels happier than before. Hence, increased savings under Prout's persuasion will never reduce social welfare. If anything, overall happiness in society will rise.

There is no doubt that, in theory at least, savings can be raised through the medium of morality. But theory is one thing, and trans-lating it into reality is another. The only way that people can be persuaded to save more is if their political leaders save more. People will be austere in their consumption, if their leaders do the same thing. Mere official preaching will not do. Nay, the leaders will have to be more austere than the people. They will have to live on the same subsistence on which the masses live. They will have to set examples before their subjects. Morality is a powerful force. But harnessing the best side of human conscience requires the leader to practice what he preaches. As is the king, so are his subjects. Hence, if leaders sacrifice their present consumption for posterity, so will the masses no matter how poor they are.

Prout's connection between morality and the savings rate is not a utopian idea. On the contrary, it is a practical and wonderful idea. For it will increase savings without reducing social happiness and harmony. Some rich people may not reduce their wasteful consumption, no matter how altruistic their leaders are. In their case, force through high taxation or confiscation may be necessary. But by and large Prout relies on human conscience and exemplary living for higher savings. A practical plan to raise savings in India, for example, has been worked out in the next chapter.

Once enough resources are generated through persuasion and even taxation, there arises the question of their utilization. Here Prout calls for balanced growth, which means allocating resources to all important sectors of the economy. Both agriculture and industry must be emphasized, and they should be developed in a way that each complements the other. Thus investment should be increased in such staples as wheat and rice; cash crops such as cotton, sugar and jute should also be promoted. Side by side, agri-based industries should be developed. This way agriculture is to complement the development of industry.

Industry, on its part, should provide fertilizers for agriculture, and modern machinery for agri-based industries. In other words, industry should be the base of agriculture, and agriculture the base of industry.

In the section on industrial policy, we found that Prout divides industry into three categories, namely the public sector producing key products, the cooperative sector comprising large scale industries producing consumption goods, and the small-scale sector comprising mainly the private industries. We also saw how the basic sector is to complement the others in a pyramidical fashion. But how are these industries to get started? Where should they be located? Answers to these questions are required in any theory of economic development.

Prout favors an industrial organization which combines elements of the present-day factories and the putting-out system which, prevailing in Europe between the 16th to the 19th century, preceded the modern factory system. In the United States also, the primary form of manufacturing organization between the 18th and 19th centuries was the putting-out system. Sarkar believes that the answer to the ubiquitous poverty in the poor nations lies not only in the modern technologies leading to high labor productivity but also in employment-generating small-scale industries located not in urban centers but in rural areas. The latest techniques can be used only in large-scale factories. They require huge investments and can be profitable usually in urban areas where skilled labor and other economies of scale are available. However, urban centers in most under-developed economies are already congested; besides they have enough unemployed people of their own, and there is no need to lure rural workers to cities. Rather, small industries should be established in the rural areas, and, as much as possible, their product should also be marketed there. Raw materials and modern machines for these industries should be supplied by the public sector [10].

As an example, take the textiles industry. Yarn and power looms can be produced in the public sector. These may in turn be leased out to weavers in villages to weave cloth in their own homes. The cloth so produced should be sold in the surrounding villages, and only the surplus in cities. If power is not available in rural areas, then hand looms should be distributed. This is just one example which can be repeated in many industries.

Let us see how this location of small industries in villages compares with the putting-out system. In this system a merchant middleman or a putter-out supplied raw materials to skilled as well as unskilled laborers who worked in their houses. Later he would collect the finished product and carry it either to the market or to another artisan for second stage of manufacturing. The putting-out set-up was prevalent in almost every industry--paper, mining, ship-building, pottery, cutlery, iron, and especially woolen and cotton textiles. The merchant middleman varied in origin as well as scale of operations. Many had a humble beginning, starting as wage earners. But most belonged to the class of merchants organized in craft guilds.

Quite often the merchant provided raw materials on credit and bought the finished goods by the piece. Occasionally, the workers bought the raw-materials and contracted for payment in wages. The same applied to the equipment, with the putter-out mostly leasing but occasionally selling it to the workers.

While workers worked mostly in their homes, usually without external supervision, with the emergence of power machinery a number of small workshops came into being in rural areas. In these workshops, eight to ten artisans worked under the supervision of a master tradesman. At times, workers would rent space in these workshops and produce goods for the putter-out. In England in early 17th century, for instance, the Earl of Shrewsbury rented out centrally located grinding wheels to master cutlers, who in their spare time subleased them to other workers.

Even when power machinery developed later and culminated in the large-scale factories in urban areas, the putting-out system worked well in rural areas for a long time. This shows that large-scale factories can coexist with profitable small-scale industries in villages. And Prout advocates the use of this latter model for rapid economic development to generate high growth and employment without large scale migration from rural to urban centers. This would avoid urban congestion and myriad related problems.

In the factory cum putting-out system mentioned above, Prout injects a dynamic role of the government which is to invest directly in modernized plants producing raw materials and equipment. The raw materials and equipment in turn should be provided to artisans in villages through the medium of a central small-scale industries agency having branches spread all over the economy. Since most workers initially will be too poor to invest money on their own, the agency should lease the equipment and raw materials to workers. Or they could purchase the machinery in installments to be deducted from their earnings. The workers could either work at home, or, if necessary, in rural workshops.

In addition to these tasks, the agency should (i) provide workers the necessary training in the use of machinery, (ii) supervise their work for quality control, at least initally, and (iii) purchase their goods on piece basis. The goods can be marketed either directly by the agency in the surrounding areas, or sold at wholesale prices to consumer-cooperatives, which in turn sell goods to final consumers. Alternatively, the agency may encourage the formation of worker's cooperatives which will lease raw materials and equipment, engage in the production process, and perform functions of quality control and the marketing of finished goods. This way workers' cooperatives may be formed for all essential commodities in rural areas. The same holds true for agri-based industries where the raw materials will come from agriculture and equipment from the small-industries agency. Small-scale industries in urban centers can also be established on the same model.

The factory cum putting-out model of economic development proposed by Prout has several advantages over the path of industrialization followed by poor nations over the last three decades. First and the obvious advantage is that no disruptive migration need occur from rural to urban areas, avoiding all concomitant problems of congestion and city pollution. The second advantage is that to the extent workers can work at home, investment in huge buildings and other infrastructure of large factories is unnecessary. As a result, substantial savings in the cost of capital can be achieved. Third, workers' cooperatives, or even workers leasing or owning their own equipment, have higher labor productivity than similar production organization based on the capitalistic firm where a producer hires workers. This point has been emphasized by Vanek in his analysis of economic development in a subsistence economy [12]. Fourth, the system will generate a relatively equitable distribution of income, and unlike the case with past developmental efforts, the poor, not just the rich, will be able to taste the fruits of economic development. Finally, with rural areas self-sufficient in essential commodities, transportation bottlenecks or disruptions caused by national disasters will not cause famines in remote places.

94

References

1. Balassa, B., and T. Bertrand, "Growth Performance of Eastern European Economies and Comparable Western European Economies," in J. Vanek (ed) *Self-Management: Economic Liberation of Man,* Penguin Books, Baltimore, 1975.

2. Batra, R. N., *The Downfall of Campitalism and Communism: A New Study of History,* Macmillan Company, London and Humanities Press, Atlantic Highlands, New Jersey, 1978.

3. _____, "Techonological Change in the Soviet Collective Farm," *American Economic Review,* 1974.

4. Commonor, B., *The Closing Circle,* Cape, London, 1963.

5. Dallas Morning News, "Congress Urged to Pass Synthetic-Fuel Developemnt Bill," June 23, 1979.

6. Domar, E. D., "The Soviet Collective Farm as a Producer Cooperative," *American Economic Review,* 1966.

7. Ehrlick, P. and A., *Population, Resources, Environment,* W. H. Freeman, San Francisco, 1972.

8. Meadows, D., *et. al., The Limits to Growth,* Earth Island, New York, 1972.

9. Mishan, E., *The Costs of Economic Growth.* Pelican, Harmondsworth, 1967.

10. Sarkar, P. R., "Problem of the Day," Ananda Marga Publication, Calcutta, 1959.

11. Vanek, J. D., *The General Theory of Labor-Managed Market Economies*, Cornell Univeristy Press, Ithaca, 1971.

12. _____, "The Subsistence Income, Effort and Developmental Potential of Labour Management and Other Economic Systems," in J. Vanek (ed) *Self-Management: Economic Liberation of Man*, Penguin Books, Baltimore, 1975.

13. Ward, B., *The Socialist Economy: A Study of Organizational Alternatives*, Random House, New York, 1967.

CHAPTER 4

ECONOMIC REFORM IN AN UNDERDEVELOPED COUNTRY WITH A SPECIAL REFERENCE TO INDIA.

One of the most glaring failures of modern economic analysis lies in devising a path of economic development which the underdeveloped countries could follow to cure the poverty of their people. Economists have recommended a wide variety of policies, some of which have even been implemented by the poor nations. Yet hardly any dent has occurred in their poverty. True, many developing nations today are semi-industrialized; some of them have even managed to move their economies into the age of highly sophisticated and computerized technologies. Yet a vast majority of their people continues to subsist under sub-human conditions.

The real cause of poverty in underdeveloped countries is the complete lack of leadership, something to which the economists have hardly paid any attention. Leadership, to me, is the most important problem of all countries, but the under-developed areas simply cannot afford the failure of their politicians. It is the job of an economist not only to prescribe suitable economic policies, but also to point out that implementation of these policies calls for honesty and integrity among the leaders. Unfortunately, economists have been lacking on both counts.

In what follows, I show how incompetent politicians and faulty economic policies have combined to produce a stagnant economy in India, which began its developmental initiative at the dawn of Independence from the British rule in 1947. And the sad story of India has been duplicated verbatim in many other developing economies. It is also shown that if the Proutist policies prescribed in the previous chapter are wholeheartedly followed, poverty in India will soon disappear. Similar policies can be applied to other underdeveloped countries as well.

There is a widespread feeling among the people that despite three decades of planning in India, malnutrition, semi-starvation, unemployment, income and wealth disparities plague the land with as much ferocity as at the dawn of Independence. Nay, things in some respects are even worse today than they were before. A candid report issued by the Reserve Bank of India in 1977 reveals that the number of poor rose sharply during the 60s. Between 1960 and 1970, the number of destitute rural households went up by 6.4 million to 27.1 million, or by a staggering 32% in just ten years. Similarly, the number of poor farmers increased by 2.2 million to 10.3 million, and the number of rural households owning nothing whatsoever rose from 750,000 to 2.1 million, or by an eyepopping 280 percent. And this in a country where the maximum wage, as noted in the previous chapter, is at least 2000 times its minimum wage.

The three decades of development have really been three decades of economic pestilence. All the industrial showpieces of modern technology bedecking the map of India pale before the monumental injustice afflicting the masses. The statistics reveal the joke that we call India's economic development, but they cannot capture the agony of hunger, the cries of the starving, the anguish of the semi-fed, semi-clothed masses, the deafening silence of rural graveyards that consume thousands of people in their teens.

What has gone wrong? What has happened to all those dreams and promises that danced before Indian society on the day of Independence?

Economists differ in their diagnosis. Some Western economists blame it all on India's religion. Thus a celebrated economist, Gunar Myrdal, contends that Hinduism and Islam are responsible for "low social and spatial mobility, little free competition in its wider sense, and great inequalities." [5, p. 104]. Allan Gruchy argues in the same vein: "Indian religion, rigid and resistant to change, constitutes a cause of economic and social inertia and an obstacle to sound national planning, because its sanction is basically irrational and opposed to a logical way of thinking." [2, p. 655]

Such arguments reveal nothing but ignorance. For one thing, is there any religion in the world that is not resistant to change? Is there any religion in the world that preaches a logical way of thinking? Why, then, is India's religion an obstacle to economic development any more than other religions?

Moreover, the question for rural masses in India is one of life and death, not one of earning a decent living. How can religious considerations come in the way of survival? Some economists argue that India discourages private investment and initiative through its excessive controls and bureaucratic red tape. There is a point in this argument, but the lack of private investment does not come close to explaining the misery of Indian masses. As in Western economies, private capital in India is reluctant to flow to industries producing necessities. It prefers to flow to luxuries, thereby diverting whatever resources are currently employed in necessities. Capitalism is not the answer to India's economic dilemmas. There is already enough of income and wealth disparity in society, and it has grown worse over the last three decades. Actually private business has flourished as never before.

While capitalism cannot solve India's problems, nor can communism, nor even democratic socialism. Even if communism could do the job, it should not be inflicted on any society. Who would like to linger through another Stalinist regime? Democratic socialism, on the other hand, combines the evils of private and State capitalism. It produces a mixed economy where relatively efficient private industries, lacking competition from inefficient state enterprises, prosper even more. Profits soar, but the masses roar.

What is then the answer? What is the prescription for India's economic ills? A diagnosis of India's sickness over the past three decades reveals that the country suffers from four tumours, namely (i) incompetent and selfish leadership, (ii) widespread corruption, (iii) the dowry system, and (iv) the caste system. Of these, which afflict entire society and hence its economy, the first tumour is cancerous and either causes the other three or directly impedes their cure. The dowry and the caste system are age-old and blaming them on post-Independence leadership may seem unfair. But they can be cured, provided those in power practice what they preach.

The Indian leaders, like their counterparts in other countries, have not been short on slogans and good intentions, only on implementation. Many scholars regcognize these tumours, but fail to comprehend their true cause.

So many Indian leaders have denounced the dowry and caste system. But how many have married out of caste? How many have rejected dowries for themselves or their sons? How many have refused to pay dowries for their daughters?

So many leaders preach honesty and integrity to others. But how many pay all their taxes? How many fail to hoard wealth? So many leaders exhort doctors to spend some time serving villages. But how many have followed their own advice?

100

So many leaders have called for ceilings on wealth. But how many have listened to their own slogans? How many have failed to profit from their self-invented loopholes?

So many leaders have asked others to consume less and save more. But how many have reduced their own consumption? How many lead austere lives themselves?

Words! Sweet words, that is all the Indian leaders offer to their people. Is there any wonder that the people emulate them, and engage in black-marketing and profiteering with abandon? Is there any wonder that there is massive corruption in society? When leaders are corrupt to the core, how can their subjects be any different? Corruption is so rampant now that you cannot get anything done without greasing a bureaucrat's palm.

India has an abundance of natural resources. But the one resource it has been lacking is moral, courageous and intelligent leadership. As a result, all other resources remain underdeveloped. India is one vast reservoir of human intellect. Scientists, economists, historians and physicians of Indian origin are prominent in so many other lands. They teach, they treat patients, they solve socio-economic problems in many other countries. Can they not do the same for their own country? They certainly can. And remember that only a fraction of India's intellectual resource is working abroad. That is why I say that India is one vast reservoir of human intellect. If it is properly harnessed, within a decade the Indian economy and society will be out of shambles. All we need to do is to divert this intellect away from selfishness to selflessness and sacrifice.

To my mind, if India is to move out of the rut of poverty, it needs a political leader who displays most of the following qualitites.

1. If he or she is married, then he (she) should have married out of cast without accepting any dowry. His (her) children should follow the same ideal. If unmarried, he (she) should be a great champion of inter-caste marriages devoid of gifts.

2. He (she) should be willing to spend long hours in villages where the masses live. He (she) may have his (her) office in a city, but frequent visits to rural areas are indispensable to keep a personal touch with the poorest people.

3. He (she) should be well-educated, pratical and honest to the core.

4. He (she) should be prepared to live on the area's minimum standard of living. His (her) duties may preclude his (her) living like a pauper, but he (she) should own no wealth. In any case, his (her) living standard should not exceed that available from the average wage.

5. Finally, he (she) should be a humanitarian with a deaf ear to vested interests and ready to introduce social and economic reforms, using force if necessary. He (she) should not cling to office, and should be ready to quit at the first indication of mass unrest in society. He (she) should be able to inspire others through his (her) austerity, integrity, intelligence and humility. In short, he (she) should take the lead in making sacrifices that others may have to make.

India's socio-economic problems are indeed gigantic. But these problems can be solved if a giant among the masses emerges to take charge and give them new hopes and directions through exemplary living. The leader must have transcended the mental weaknesses. He must have boundless love for the masses and not for the office.

Is it possible to find such a leader in today's India? The answer is yes. For leaders emerge in response to urgent cries of downtrodden humanity. And there is no doubt that the suffering in India has been long and real. One after another incompetent and self-centered persons have been at the top. As a result, the chaos, the unrest and unsecurity that surfeit society today have become irreversible. But before long a new leader should emerge to wrest the initiative and provide new hope to glum eyes.

It is this incompetent leadership, which has thus far followed toothless and faulty economic policies, that is solely responsible for India's economic problems. Prout's economic system, presented in the previous chapter, is designed to increase savings and labor productivity, eliminate injustices and provide at least minimum living standards to all workers as well as the handicapped. India, therefore, needs a strong leader and a five point economic program that flows from Proutist guidelines.

(i) Every rural worker should receive a monthly income of at least 200 rupees, and an urban worker at least 300 rupees; but no wage should exceed 2,000 rupees per month; these wages should, of course, be adjusted periodically with inflation;

(ii) No family should own more than one house or residential property exceeding 60,000 rupees in rural areas, whichever is higher in value. Similar ceilings on urban tangible property, to be obtained from my formula developed in the previous chapter, should be enforced in cities;

(iii) No able-bodied capitalist should own stocks and bonds exceeding the area's wealth-ceiling on cash, and the surplus stock should be properly distributed among workers;

(iv)   Appropriate land-ceilings should be enforced in, agriculture

(v)   Finally all private firms competing with public firms in key industries producing inter-mediate goods such as steel, coal, yarn, among others, should be nationalized and assigned to autonomous bodies which should run them on the same basis as private firms facing competition are run.   No one should be given the luxury of job security just for seniority.   Only performance should count.

FEASIBILITY OF REFORMS

Let us now see if the reforms advocated above are feasible.   Some economists suggest that measures aimed at reducing income inequalitites induce a decline in savings and hence in the economy's rate of growth.   Others suggest that a national minimum wage should not be introduced in India, or it should be low enough to be compatible with the capacity of private industries to pay it. I will presently argue that the Proutist reforms presented above are not only feasible, but they will also reduce social misery and stimulate eco-nomic growth.

As early as 1948, a minimum wage act was introduced to set minimum wages for certain industries.   It was a landmark act designed to prevent the "sweating" of unskilled labor by unscrupulous employers.   It had good intentions, but, as usual, its intentions were not translated into realtiy, especially when it was applied to industries with no or weak labor unions.   The Act soon became a farce, and the employers continued to pay pitiful wages determined by conditions of low demand and excessive supply of unskilled workers.   In any case the 1948 act did not call for a national minimum wage.

ECONOMIC REFORM IN AN UNDERDEVELOPED COUNTRY

Ever since, the concept of minimum wage has been debated from time to time. It was taken up by the 15th Indian Labor Conference which called for the fixation of a standard wage ensuring the minimum human needs of an industrial worker. The minimum wage was to provide for a daily diet of 2700 calories, 72 yards of clothing for the family per annum and a house conforming to the minimum rent charged by the government in its subsidized housing schemes. While the labor conference provided guidelines for fixing minimum wages in industries, it stopped short of recommending a standard need-based wage applicable to all sectors. In other words, it left room for differential minimum wages in different sectors of production.

In 1966, the government appointed a National Commission on Labor to look anew at the wage structure. The commission presented its report in 1969, recommending a need-based minimum wage, regardless of the industry's capacity to pay. As with the Labor Conference, it also did not advocate a national minimum wage.

Recently the government appointed a Study Group on Wages, Incomes and Prices, which presented its report in May 1978. After examining all pros and cons, the study group has indeed called for the fixation of a national minimum wage, which is to equal 150 rupees and is to be enforced in seven years.

The study group has moved in the right direction. The current wage structure is indefensible on all conceivable grounds, and as the study group points out, "The wage strucure abounds in disparities, distortions and anomalies between the government, public and private sectors and within each sector itself." [7, p. 19]. When an office clerk in some firms earns more than a deputy secretary to the government or a doctor, you know there is something wrong with the system.

But while the concept of a uniform nationwide minimum wage has its merit, the great difference in rural and urban areas cannot be ignored. The argument of the 1966 National Commission on Labor is quite convincing in this regard. In the Commission's view, "a national minimum wage in the sense of a uniform minimum monetary remuneration for the country as a whole is neither feasible nor desirable. If one is fixed, the dangers are that there will be areas which will not afford the minimum if the minimum is worked out somewhat optimistically. And if calculations are allowed to be influenced by what a poorer region or industry can pay, the national minimum will not be worth enforcing." [6, p. 234]

In view of the internal merit of the minimum wage and wide regional disparities in the cost of living, I have called for a dual minimum wage system, with one wage applying to rural areas and the other to urban areas. In the rural sector, I recommend a minimum wage of 200 rupees per month for any worker 18 years or above. This is to apply to continuous employment. For day-to-day work, the minimum rural wage should be 8 rupees per eight-hour day, on the principle that full time work in India usually calls for working 25 days a month. This will then produce a monthly income of 200 rupees.

In the urban sector, the minimum wage should be 300 rupees per month or 12 rupees per eight-hour day. It should be remembered that these are minimum wages only for unskilled work. For skilled work, wages should be higher, depending on conditions of demand and supply. But in no case should they be less than the minimum wage.

Let me now compare my dual-wage system with the one recommended by the study group which calls for a national uniform minimum wage of 150 rupees, beginning with 100 rupees in the first year, but rising to its equivalent in real terms over seven years.

First of all, the study group glosses over all the valid arguments against a uniform minimum wage in India. Second, its minimum wage is a joke; it is far below subsistence. In a recent paper, Subbarayudu argues that the need-based minimum wage today is about 300 rupees per month [9, p. 990] and that is what I have recommended for urban areas. However, the same need-based minimum wage in rural areas approximates 200 rupees. And the study group recommends half of this amount in the first year in both villages and cities.

To the study group, a minimum wage above 100 rupees would cause great dislocations in industry. I say that if an industry cannot even pay the need-based wage to all, then it must be paying excessive and undeserving wages to its white-collar workers and executives. To be feasible, the minimum wage must be combined with the maximum wage. Based on the decimal-scale of income distribution described in the previous chapter, the maximum wage should be no more than 2000 rupees per month. And the maximum should apply to all sectors.

Let us see if this egalitarian wage-structure is feasible. Hereafter, I make the following assumptions for my analysis.

(i) Top 5 percent of households consume 30 percent of national income in India.

(ii) Each household, on the average, is a family of 6 persons, including children and other dependents.

(iii) Bottom 20 percent of households consume 4

percent of national income.

I have made these assumptions on the basis of previous studies of family size and income inequities. The two assumptions about income distribution derive from the Lorenz curve drawn by Rajinder Koshal [3, p. 141]. The studies of India's income distribution conducted by Ojha and Bhatt, ECAFE and the NCAER more or less support these assumptions which convey the indisputable fact that India suffers from pathetic income disparities. (See Mahajan [5] who cites these studies). The average size of a family of 6 also draws some support from existing literature. The numbers I have chosen may not please everybody, but the point that I make below stands on its own.

The Central Statistical Organization (CSO) has recently released "quick estimates" of national income for the year 1977-78 [1]. According to these estimates, national income in the year in question stood at 822,650 millions of rupees. If 30% of that income went to income earners in the top 5% bracket, then the richest persons earned 246,795 million rupees. With a population estimate of 630 million and a household of 6, the number of the top 5% families was 5.25 million. The average income of the top 5% families, therefore, equalled 47,008 rupees per year. This income is almost twice the maximum wage of 24,000. If such maximum were to be enforced, roughly half of the income going to the top 5 percent bracket of population would be freed for other use. Let us say the income so released is 122,000 million rupees.

On the other end of the income ladder, 20 percent of population earned a lowly 4 percent of income. This means that in 1977-78, 21 million families earned 32,906 million, or an average of 1,567 rupees per year. If the minimum wage of 200 is enforced, an average family at the lowest income level will recieve an extra 833 rupees, or a total of 17,493 million, which is easily covered by the income released by the top 5 percent bracket. Even if the minimum wage for all workers is 300 rupees per month, the additional income of the poorest people will add to only 42,693 million, which is far below the released income. Thus, it is clear that my need-based concept of minimum wage is easily feasible, provided the maximum wage is enforced at the same time.

The mini-maxi wage structure that I have recommended, while reducing income disparities, will increase savings, thereby promoting growth. And as growth occurs, both the minimum and the maximum wage can be raised.

Let us examine the question of savings more carefully. The richest people in society are supposed to have the highest propensity to save. The average rate of household saving in India has been around 5 percent. The rich waste a lot of money, and they may not necessarily save at a higher rate. In fact, Raj Kumar Sen has recently argued that reducing income inequalities in India will not reduce savings [8, p. 97]. However, the wage-structure that I have suggested will actually raise total savings.

Suppose the propensity to save of the rich is, say, as high as 20 percent. Any higher figure is unlikely. And suppose, the top five percent of income earners save nothing after the maximum wage is imposed. Then the total household savings will decline by 49,359 million. But the income released by them was 122,000 million, and that transfered to the poorest people was at the most 42,693 million. If the poor consume all they earn, even then the net income released (after deducting the saving loss and the income transfer) will be 29,948 million. Hence total savings in the economy will rise by this last amount.

The following objections may be raised to my analysis. To begin with, not all the income of the rich comes from wage earning. A part of it, and a substantial part, derives from property. A mere imposition of a maximum wage will not then cut their earnings by nearly half, as I have calculated above, so that the net savings may or may not rise. Excessive incomes from property will have to be abolished from my recommendation of ceilings on wealth. And the workers will then earn not only a minimum wage but also some income from wealth, for stocks and bonds should be distributed among laborers. The implementation of this wealth distribution may take two or three years, and during the transition much of the income from stocks and bonds will accrue to the State, thereby raising total savings and hence growth. In that interregnum, the government will also be able to provide training to representatives of workers in the management of industries.

What about the self-employed in rural and urban areas? Rich farmers, store-owners, physicians, etc., are self employed, and their incomes may escape the maximum ceiling. This will be a real problem, especially when the tax system in India is notorious for its ineffectiveness. This dilemma could be tackled in various ways. Since the government will have little need to enforce the tax laws over wage-earners, it could concentrate on the self-employed and collect the extra income through taxation. Recognizing that some income will still escape the tax-collector, the government could impose stiff excise taxes on luxury goods bought by the remaining rich, thereby collecting a portion of their extra incomes. Finally, the government could fix lower prices to be charged by the rich sections of the self-employed.

Some may object to my assumptions. The top 5

percent of households may be receiving less than 30 percent of national income. Maybe the family size of a wage earner is not 6 but 5, or even 4. Maybe! But my point still remains. For no matter what the assumptions are, the income released by the top bracket will be several times the income transfer required to raise consumption of the poorest people to the minimum level. And if the released income, for some reason, is not enough, then the maximum wage should be reduced further to, say, 9 times the minimum wage. For providing the minimum needs of each and every one is the most urgent task facing society.

I may add, however, that my estimate of the income freed from the upper-income group may be on the low side. For I have examined only that group whose average income is about 4,000 rupees per month. There must be another large group with monthly incomes between 2,000 to 4,000. Given the maximum wage limit, this group will also free income that could be used either for raising the incomes of the poorest people or for capital formation. Thus the mini-maxi structure flowing from Proutist principles will not only reduce income disparity, not only reduce social misery on a vast scale, but will also promote healthy economic growth.

The anlaysis presented above has been conducted in terms of the Indian economy and society. But a careful examination shows that most, if not all, other underdeveloped economies suffer from similar ills. Hence the Proutist policies prescribed in this chapter will work for other developing economies as well. There will be quantitative differences, but the essential tenor of my argument will be unchanged. Thus a mini-maxi wage structure can also be designed for other poverty-stricken areas to promote savings, economic growth and social well-being.

PROUT: THE ALTERNATIVE TO CAPITALISM AND MARXISM

References

1. Estimates of National Product, Saving and Capital Formation, 1977-78, *Eastern Economist,* January 19, 1978.

2. Gruchy, Allan, *Comparative Economic Systems,* Houghton Mifflin, Boston, 1977.

3. Koshal, Rajinder, "Socialist Society: An Analysis of India's Economic Policy," in *India's Economic Problems,* editied by J. S. Uppal, Tata McGraw-Hill, New Delhi, 1975.

4. Mahajan, O. P., "Economic Growth and Income Distribution in India: Trends Prospects and Policy Implications," *Indian Economic Journal,* October 1978.

5. Myrdal, Gunar, *Asian Drama, An Inquiry Into the Poverty of Nations,* Vol. I., Pantheon Books, New York, 1968.

6. *Report of the National Commission on Labour,* Ministry of Labour and Employment and Rehabilitation, Government of India, 1968.

7. *Report of the Study Group on Wages, Incomes and Prices,* Bureau of Public Enterprises, Ministry of Finance, Government of India, 1978.

8. Sen, Raj Kumar, "Our Level of Living and Savings During the Plans," *Indian Economic Journal,* Vol. 25, October 1977.

9. Subbarayudu, C., "National Minimum Wage: A Necessary Concept," *Eastern Economist,* November 17, 1978.

CHAPTER 5

ECONOMIC REFORM IN THE WEST WITH
SPECIAL REFERENCE TO THE UNITED STATES

In the previous chapter, I have diagnosed the socio-economic problems facing an underdeveloped country such as India, and then prescribed various Proutist policies to solve these ills. The policies called for some unorthodox measures along with honesty and integrity on the part of leaders.

This chapter deals with Western societies which are also facing problems unprecedented in recent history. The West is today afflicted by inflation, unemployment, high crime, pornography, drug and alcoholic addiction, social indiscipline, and so on. With the developed countries, as with developing countries, the basic cause of social dilemmas is the same--the total lack of leadership. "As is the king, so are his subjects" is a well-known adage that held true in the past and is holding true today. Scholars now often lament that if the people only controlled their gluttony and their appetite for ever-new gadgets, the Western systems will come back to order. They blame it all on the selfishness of the people. How myopic are they though? The people have grown selfish, because their leaders have grown super-selfish; the people have become greedy, because their leaders have become super-greedy.

There is little doubt that today, in terms of materialism, greed and guile, politicians in the West, as in all other societies, excell their citizens. And this is the basic cause of all social dilemmas. Once the politician keeps his own house in order, once he practices what he prescribes, the ills of society will disappear.

In the following pages, I examine the problems facing the United States, which at present is the most prominent country in Western society. I then

show that only the adoption of the Proutist economic system is the proper solution. This may call
for radical changes in thinking, but then unprecedented problems call for unprecedented reforms,
which are applicable to all Western economies.

EVOLUTION OF THE U.S. SOCIETY

Ever since birth, the U.S. society has been
evolving through the age of acquisiters, that is
to say, people of acquisitive mentality, the
wealthy, have had the dominant voice in most
socio-economic affairs in American society right
from its beginning [see 1. Ch. 9]. Prior to the
Civil War, wealthy landlords were the dominant
force in the U.S., but following that war their
place has been taken by wealthy industrialists,
bankers and merchants. Therefore, in one form or
another, the rich have been at the top of the
social hierarchy in America. (For further details
about the acquisitive mind, see Ch. 6 of this
book.)

Whenever the wealthy rule society, the political and administrative system is highly decentralized. This can be substantiated from six thousand
years of human history in many civilizations. The
reason why the rich hate a centralized political
system is the danger that an absolute ruler, if it
suited his purpose, could force them to give away
their wealth to the poor. No one is more aware of
this hazard of a centralized system than the class
of acquisiters. Hence whenever the latter are
predominant in society, the political system is
decentralized in the extreme.

What aquisiters know best is how to make
money. They are not adept in the art of writing
catchy theories, which can be provided only by
intellectuals. Therefore in the age of acquisiters, intellectuals, in the interest of their
careers, devise such theories as justify the rule

of wealth. How they do it depends on trends of the times. During Feudalism, when wealthy landlords ruled all over Europe, religion was a pervasive force in society. Hence the then intellectuals justified the rule of landlords in terms of a God-created order. During capitalism, however, intellectuals speak in terms of logic and rationality. Today the rule of wealth is justified in terms of economic efficiency and high growth for which only the rich are supposed to be responsible.

When acquisiters rule society, their thinking, their mentality gradually comes to infect everyone else. Everybody wants what the wealthy want; everybody wants to become rich quickly, because everyone can see that money brings power and prestige. Hence in the age of acquisiters, people slowly get infected by the excessive materialim of the ruling class.

The first to get infected by the acquisitive instinct are the very intellectuals who support the system through their theories. Such people may be called intellectual acquisiters to distinguish them from "pure" acquisiters who are incapable of originating subtle ideas. At the beginning of the age of acquisiters, pure acquisiters remain unchallenged in society; but towards the end of this age, social supremacy passes into the hands of the intellectual acquisiter. No age lasts forever, as is shown in the next chapter. The fact that the influence of pure wealth loses ground to the wealthy intellectual itself indicates that the age of pure wealth is on the decline.

During the capitalistic phase of the age of the wealthy (the previous age of the wealthy in the West occurred during Feudalism), we find that pure acquisiters dominated society until 1929, when the U.S. and other parts of the Western world were hit by the severest of all economic depressions. The entire capitalist colossus was then on the verge of collapse. The very foundations of Western civilization were then shaken.

Until the Great Crash of 1929, the popular ideology was that the government should keep its hands off the economy and other affairs of society. This is called the neoclassical economic doctrine, which is precisely the one most acceptable to the pure acquisiter. In the aftermath of the Great Depression, however, the sickly economic system turned to intellectuals for survival. It is at such precarious times that a brilliant economist, John Maynard Keynes, reexamined the economic theory, and came to the rescue of the system. Instead of a hands-off policy, Keynes called for constant governmental watch on the economy. His policies called for radical changes in the thinking of economists and social scientists.

At first the Keynesian thought met with hostile reaction from scholars as well as their wealthy patrons. But then came the second world war during which the governments were forced to incur high budget deficits, which were precisely what Keynes had recommended to solve the problem of unemploymnet. During the war, the Western economies quickly moved out of depression, thereby proving that Keynes was right after all. Since then Keynesian economics has become the accepted doctrine of the Western world.

Keynes gave high respect to the interventionist sentiment. Ever since the Great Depression, it is the intellectual acquisiter who has been ruling in the United States. An intellectual loves to intervene with the society. His forte is in devising new and new theories. Whether they are practical or not, he does not care. All he cares is that they should be lofty or catchy.

An intellectual acquisiter combines the hypocricy of the pure intellectual with the greed of the pure acquisiter. That is why when the intellectual acquisiter comes to power, he, along with the rest of society, denounces the greed and income sources of the pure acquisitor, while forgetting his own greed. That is why incomes from high profits are today denounced in America, but high incomes from other sources gain hardly the same attention. Profit today is a 'dirty' word, but what about the high incomes and greed of today's intellectuals. The politicians go hoarse in condemning the "obscene" profits of oil companies; but what about their own "obscene" incomes.

It is the intellectual acquisiter who today runs the Western world. That is why we find that all democracies are caught in the stranglehold of countless rules and regulations. For it is in the arena of impractical ideas that most intellectuals thrive. Problems require fundamental reforms. But the intellectual acquisiter, lacking the strength that comes from self-discipline and austerity, calls only for patch-work policies designed to patch the torn system. Today he is putting patches on patches, introducing new regulations without bothering to see if the new rules contradict his earlier rules.

Many economists today, as perhaps in the past, are intellectual acquisiters. One can understand the greed of those who justify capitalism in the unimpeachable garb of individual liberty and justice. For they openly proclaim avarice as a virtue. But what about the greed of the sharpest critics of capitalism! What about the critics of the affluent society! They too have made fortunes by pouring their hearts out for the poor. On closer scrutiny, therefore, we find that some scholars have made their millions in support of capitalism, while others have done the same through their critiques of the capitalist order. Thus most prominent writers, liberal or conservative, are intellectual acquisiters. Hence the policies they prescribe can never solve the problems. They are not interested in solving problems: They are interested in making money, by prescribing myopic policies designed to preserve social supremacy of the few millionaires.

CURRENT ECONOMIC THOUGHT

The neoclassical economic ideology, with its prescription for laissez faire, drew its inspiration from the writings of Adam Smith, who is known as the father of economics. The neoclassical thought believed that there is an automatic mechanism that corrects every problem in a capitalist economy. For instance, if there is large scale unemployment, then wages would fall and businessmen would be induced to hire more workers. On the other side, fewer workers would offer their services with falling wages, and a point would come when the increased demand for labor would match the contracted labor supply. In other words, all those willing to work would eventually find employment, and unemployment would disappear. All this would occur through the flexibility of the wage rate which falls whenever unemployment is high. In the neoclassical view, therefore, unemployment persists when the government artificially keeps the wage rate high through minimum wage laws. Eliminating the minimum wage is then the neoclassical solution for unemployment. In other words, the system works fine as long as the government does not interfere with it.

Not only does the capitalist system automatically solve all its problems, but, to neoclassical economists, it is also efficient. Their argument usually proceeds in this way. Assuming that consumers and businessmen are unable to influence market prices, consumers, in their own interest, allocate their expenditure on various goods in a way that their utility is maximized. This process of utility maximization ensures that each consumer would like to buy high quality goods at the lowest possible price. Knowing this, businessmen, facing keen comptition from each other, scramble to satisfy the consumers' needs by supplying the best-quality products at the lowest possible price. This they have to do in their own interest which is in the attainment of maximum profits. It is this self interest which induces businessmen to hire resources from households such that they are put to the most efficient uses. In other words, the very ojective of profit maximization induces the producers to hire factors of production in such a way that each factor is paid the value of his marginal product. Since the reward depends on the marginal product, every worker is induced to work to his maximum potential. A system that preserves such incentives must therefore be the most efficient.

The neoclassical defense of capitalism is quite simple and appealing. The system is shown to be working smoothly because of the self-interest and greed of each and every person. There is a minor problem though. And that is that the self-interest of businessmen forces them to be predators. Like bigger fish gobbling up the smaller fish, the more successful businesses have the tendency to gobble up the less successful ones. To reduce competition, bigger corporations tend to take over the smaller corporations, because competition is the bane of profits. Hence the neoclassical thought, which has been assuming keen competition among businessmen for more than two centuries, is blind to economic reality, which is one of monopolies and oligopolies. Consumers are still price-takers, but producers, in almost all industries, have become price makers.

In 1929 when the capitalist economies

collapsed, the gap between economic theory and economic reality had never been greater. While the economic reality was one of monopolies, oligopolies, speculation and extreme concentration of wealth in a few hands, economic theory assumed a world in which competing businessmen scramble for consumers' money to generate an economy where everyone seeking a job finds work at a wage equalling his contribution to social product. The average economist of the time either lived in a fool's paradise, or chose to ignore reality in the interest of his own career. It is not that industrial giants had emerged all at once. Economists had plenty of time to examine the observed phenomena of the bulging economic concentration which had begun right after the Civil War. In fact so many businessmen had conspired to restrict competition among themselves that the U.S. Congress had to pass the Sherman Anti-Trust Act in 1889.

In 1934, Mathew Josephson wrote a book entitled *The Robber Barrons,* a title he used to describe the behavior of some wealthy businessmen who dominated their industries toward the end of the nineteenth century. He reserved his title for such men as John D. Rockefeller in oil, Andrew Carnegie in steel, J. P. Morgan in banking among many others. What they did to control their industries shines in the history of shoddy tactics.[1] The point is that their activities were well-known, but despite this, economists continued to present the corporate executive as a tireless and honest worker striving to meet consumer needs at lowest possible prices; and many continue to do so today.

As a result of such glaring misconception, the economic profession was ill-prepared for the onslaught of the Great Depression. An economic epidemic of unprecedented proportions had hit the Western world, with economists watching it helplessly for want of proper theory. As stated earlier, it was left to Keynes to provide a new theory, which rescued the system from collapse.

Keynes began by reexamining the neoclassical theory of employment, which had held that the capitalist economy automatically moves towards full employment, given a flexible wage system. He argued that in the event of unemployment, a declining wage rate need not induce businessmen to hire more workers, for the wage rate not only enters into calculations of cost, but for the system as a whole it provides a base for aggregate demand. Thus a falling wage rate also signifies a falling demand in the economy. In such an atmosphere, businessmen are unlikely to hire more workers.

Having demolished the neoclassical logic, Keynes set out to formulate his own theory of employment. Until the appearance of Keynesian theory, economists had pinned their faith in J. B. Say's law, asserting that supply creates its own demand, so that general overproduction or excess capacity can never occur in the eonomy. Keynes turned Say's law around and argued that demand creates its own supply. If there is sufficient demand, then businessmen will hire workers to produce goods to meet that demand. Therefore if all those willing to work at the market wage are to be employed, then the aggregate demand for all goods and services should be adequate to match the level of goods and services produced by the fully employed workers. Hence the government's economic policy should be such as to maintain a level of aggregate demand commensurate with the full-employment aggregate supply.

Aggregate demand consists of businessmen's spending on investment goods, such as machinery, and the expenditure on consumption goods by private consumers and government. Therefore the government can affect the aggregate demand by

121

adopting policies affecting the aggregate spending. Here Keynes makes a distinction between monetary and fiscal policies. Monetary policy deals with the aggregate supply of money. Keynes argues that expanding money supply stimulates business investment, and conversely. Fiscal policy, by contrast, deals with the government budget which involves the determination of total spending by the government and its tax revenue. Keynes contends that a budget deficit leads to an expansion in aggregate demand, whereas a surplus results in a corresponding contraction.

The economic policies open to society are now clear. In times of depression, when aggregate demand falls short of potential output commensurate with full employment, both monetary and fiscal policies should be expansionary. In other words, the government should then (i) expand the supply of money and/or (ii) incur budget deficit by increasing government spending or reducing taxes or both. By the same token, in times of inflation, when aggregate demand exceeds the output level consistent with full employment, monetary and fiscal policies should be contractionary.

What Keynes recommended was no less than a revolutionary change in the socio-economic thought. And predictably his ideas met a hostile reception: Whenever new ideas emerge, they have to fight with the old. The neoclassical economic philiosophy, entrenched in the social thought ever since Adam Smith wrote his *Wealth of Nations* in 1776, had all along argued for laissez faire, which also meant a balanced budget policy. And here was Keynes challenging the entire conventional wisdom, pleading for the State to adopt the apparently imprudent policy of budget deficits.

Moreover, Keynes argued that the government would have to keep a ceaseless watch over the economy. This is because investment is a double edged weapon, raising aggregate demand in the short run but increasing aggregate supply in the long run. This means that the government will constantly have to monitor the economy to ensure against the possiblity of general overproduction.

At first, the government was reluctant to follow Keynsian prescriptions. But then, as stated earlier, came the second world war, which forced huge budget deficits on warring nations where unemployment soon disappeared. Keynes was proved right after all. Keynsian economics has become the accepted doctrine ever since.

Keynesian prescriptions have not gone unchallanged of course. The most serious challenge has come form Milton Friedman who argues that the government is not intelligent enough to fine-tune as giant an entity as the economy. In his view, the Great Depression, and for that matter other depressions of the 19th and 20th centuries, ocurred because of the government's meddling with the country's supply of money. Every depression was preceeded by a decline in the growth of money, resulting thereby in an artificial decline in aggregate demand and hence in unemployment. The government, according to Friedman, should limit itself to maintaining a steady rate of growth of money, matching the rate of growth of economic activity. This, in the long run, will ensure full employment without inflation. As regards budgetary policy, Friedman argues again for a fixed rule whereby the government keeps the so called full employment budget in balance. According to this rule, after the government has decided what it wants to spend, it should set its taxes at such a rate that its budget would be in balance if the labor force were fully employed. If the economy were operating at anywhere less than full employment, taxes would fall short, causing a budget deficit. At any point above full employment, the budget would be in surplus because of higher tax receipts. This rule then amounts to long run balance in government's budget, although in the short run there could be budget deficits or surpluses.

The main difference between Keynes and Friedman about economic policy, therefore, is that while Keynes likes the government to actively intervene in the economy, following appropriate monetary and fiscal policies, Friedman siding with neoclassical economists, likes the government to stay out of the system and to conduct its economic policy according to clearly announced rules. The economic profession today is divided between these two approaches.

During the three decades following the Second World War, both approaches have been followed by the government in the United States, and both have met with dubious success.

The most clear-cut case where economic policy in the United States relfected Keynesian prescriptions occurred in 1964, when income tax rates for individuals and corporations were lowered chiefly to stimulate aggregate demand. In 1964, unemployment hovered around 5.7 percent; by 1966, it had come down to 4 percent, which is considered to be full employment. Clearly the expansionary fiscal policy had succeeded in eliminating unemployment. The rate of economic growth also surged from 4 percent in 1964 to 6 percent by 1966.

The vigorous economic activity triggered by the tax cut resulted in an increase in inflation. Between 1961-64, prices had been rising at the rate of 1 to 1.5 percent. But between 1966 and 69, their rate of increase varied from 3 to 5.4 percent, almost three times the earlier rate. In retrospect we find that in order to finance the budget deficits resulting from the permanent tax cut of 1964, the Federal Reserve Bank, which is responsible for the conduct of monetary policy, had expanded the money supply at a faster rate. In the face of rising inflation, the Fed reduced the growth of money supply from a rate of 4.8 percent in 1964 to 1.5 percent in 1966. The result was a credit crunch, a rise in interest rates, and a mini recession in 1967.

But then came high government spending and expansionary monetary policy caused by the Vietnam War which by 1966 had moved into full gear. By 1967 money supply began to grow at the annual rate of 7 percent, and soon inflation and employment shot up again. The government reacted by introducing fiscal restraint through a temporary "tax surcharge" in 1968. This was meant to be a restrictive fiscal policy on the lines recommended by Keynes, but it was not accompanied by monetary restraint. The result was that inflation remained strong despite the fiscal restraint. Critics of Keynes pointed to this as an example of the failure of Keynesian policies. But Keynes had been followed only half-heartedly, because fiscal prudence was not matched by monetary prudence.

By 1969 unemployment was down to 3.5 percent, while inflation raged at the then intolerable level of 5.4 percent. Keynesian policies had led to growing disenchantment among the economists. The time was ripe for the rise of Friedman, for his monetarism and for his gradualist approach aiming to restrain money growth over long time.

Both monetary and fiscal policies became restrictive in 1969. It was decided that the fight against inflation should be slow but steady. However, money growth was reduced sharply from a rate of 8.1 percent at the end of 1968 to 2.3 percent at the end of 1969; in 1970 the rate averaged at 5 percent. But despite this sharp monetary restraint, inflation actually went up from 5.4 percent in 1969 to 5.9 percent in 1970. Unemployment also went up from 3.5 percent to 4.9 percent. Friedman's policy had been tried, but it had only succeeded in raising unemployment without reducing inflation. By 1972 inflation did come down to 3.3 percent, but unemployment rose to 5.6 percent.

Inflation and unemployment, which had been twin evils of the capitalist economies throughout the 1970s, show no sign of abatement in the 1980s. The policy maker faces a painful dilemma. Both Keynesian activism and Friedman's prudent monetary restraint have been tried, but without much success. The system has developed so many inherent contradictions because of the greed and hypocrisy of the dominant class of intellectual acquisiters that any external shock can send it reeling for cover.

One such shock came in 1973 when OPEC quadrupled the price of oil which most Western countries import. And inflation in the United States hit a post-war record of 11 percent in 1974, along with an unemployment of 5.6 percent. It may be mentioned here that money supply during that year grew only at the rate of 4 percent. Not since the Second World War had the West faced such crisis which would see unemployment surge to as high as 8.5 percent. In response the government followed the Keynesian prescriptions again. Taxes were reduced in 1975 leading to the highest post-war budget deficit of 59 billion dollars, while money supply was allowed to grow at the rate of 5.3 percent which is moderate in comparison to rates of 8 to 10 percent experienced between 1977-79. Today inflation is at 15 percent whereas unemployment hovers around 7 percent. And there is no end in sight to the double-edged bite of soaring stagflation.

WHAT IS WRONG?

Economists today display helplessness before the monster of stagflation. They seem to know what has caused it, but they offer few cures. I will presently argue that the current economic thought is not only myopic in its diagnosis of the economic ills, but is also faulty in its prescriptions. But first let us see what the majority of scholars believes today.

Most experts currently blame stagflation on Big Government, which to them means high government spending, high taxes, high growth of money supply, and a maze of federal rules and regulations. High government spending causes excessive waste of society's scarce resources, high taxes destroy incentives for businessmen to invest and for people to work hard, high growth of money means too much money chasing too few goods, and excessive regulation imposes unnecessary costs on private producers. All these repercussions of big government discourage production of goods while stoking the fires of inflation. The cures for the malady of stagflation, therefore, lie in lower government spending, reduced taxes, abolition of regulations, and restraint over the growth of money supply over a long period of time.

This in short is the majority opinion among economists today. A recent issue of *Time* magazine, August 27, 1979, clearly articulates this sentiment in an essay entitled "To Set the Economy Right: The Rising Rebel Cry for Less Government, More Incentive and Investment." The title of this essay aptly conveys the current thinking.

It is hard to disagree with the battle cry against Big Government. The current diagnosis of the scholars is correct as far as it goes. But it is myopic. It fails to ask the question: is there anything in the economic system that produces the need for Big Government? Is there anything in capitalism that periodically brings it running to the government for help?

In response to such questions, economists put the blame on politicians, as if the politicians have a vested interest in a battered economy. The fact is that capitalism cannot exist without social sanction of everyone's unlimited right to property, and that right is rooted in the Constitution itself. The real problem, as I will shortly demonsrate, lies in this sanction of property rights and the concomitant intstitutions.

It is true that huge budget deficits accompanied by excessive monetary growth are among the major causes of inflation. This phenomenon of money creation to finance budget deficits is called deficit financing. But why has the system needed such deficit financing for more than a decade? The answer lies in unemployment. In 1975, the year of the largest post war budget deficit of 59 billion dollars, unemployment stood at 8.5 percent along with an inflation rate of 9 percent. The government responded with increased deficit financing and by 1979 unemployment was down to 6 percent while inflation raged at 13 percent. But suppose the government had listened to the monetarists and kept money growth to say 4 percent per year; inflation would have been controlled but unemployment would have skyrocketed to somewhere above 10 percent. Six million people were unemployed in 1979. With unemployment exceeding 10 percent, more than 10 million people would have been out of work. The reality is that monopoly capitalism simply needs deficit financing for survival: No system founded on pure self-interest and materialsm can endure for long if millions of its citizens are unemployed. And the economists today readily concede that efforts to control deficit financing over long periods will definitely create large-scale unemployment. But they argue that this is a painful pill which the economy, especially the politician, must swallow to control inflation. What kind of cure is that where millions of people must undergo intolerable sufferings so that the system, inherently unstable, is brought back to order?

What is wrong with the economy, therefore, is not deficit financing, but the nature of monopoly capitalism which has needed large budget deficits to keep the level of unemployment from rising to "dangerous" levels. In the next section I show that the need for deficit financing is rooted in the capitalist system itself.

UNLIMITED PRIVATE PROPERTY AND STAGFLATION

It has been observed by experts that of every dollar earned in the United States about 30 cents go to the owners of capital and 70 cents to laborers. This division of income between labor and capital has displayed a market stability over the last hundred years. In this analysis, the whole population is divided between workers and proprietors, with the latter owning much of the property such as stocks, bonds and real estate. Thus roughly 30 percent of national income accrues to the owners of property and 70 percent to owners of labor.

Let us now consider a simple numerical example. Suppose the economy needs to employ one more worker to be at the level of full employment. Suppose the average annual wage of a full-time job is 100 dollars, and suppose a budget deficit of 100 dollars would increase aggregate demand also by only 100 dollars. In other words, for simplicty assume that Keynesian multiplier is equal to one, although in reality it is greater than one under conditions of unemployment. But I am only trying to make a point here and not to produce an exact analysis, which will come later.

Given these assumptions, a 100 dollars of budget deficit will increase national income also by 100 dollars, as producers match the increased aggregate demand of 100 dollars by expanding their production by the same amount. Now the question is: Will that one unemployed person get a full-time job? The answer is no.

If a worker is hired to expand output, then of the additional national income of $100, 70 will go to that worker, with the rest going to the employer in terms of say profits even though the producer is already well-off and does not need the additional money. In any case, the government policy was meant only to help the unemployed. Since the wage rate for a full time job is also $100, but the worker ends up getting only $70, it is clear that the worker will not be fully-employed. His job will be only a part-time job; in order that he gets a full-time job the government's deficit will have to be greater than $100. It will have to be roughly $143 out of which 70 percent will go to the worker to produce a $100 job and $43 will go to the employer. This $43 is the price that the system will have to pay to the already affluent industrialist so that he offers work to the unemployed worker.

What does this simple numerical illustration tell us? It tells us that since 30 percent of all national income goes to owners of property, regardless of whether they work, and since the property owners chiefly control the means of production, the government has to generate ever-increasing budget deficits to maintain high levels of employment. The objective of deficit financing is to help the unemployed, but the economic system is such that the deficit ends up increasing incomes of both the jobless workers and the affluent industrialists. Since it ends up enriching the rich also, a given level of deficit produces insufficient jobs for the jobless. Stated differently, to sustain high levels of employment, larger than necessary budget deficits have to be maintained by the government. And these deficits in turn cause inflation. Hence the real cause of stagfltion, of the twins of inflation and unemployment, is the social sanction of unlimited private property, whereby everyone is free to amass as much wealth as possible regardless of how much he already has. Big government is not the cause of stagflation, only its symptom. The main culprits are monopoly capitalism and extreme inequities in the ownership of wealth that create the need for Big Government to sustain adequate levels of employment.

PROUTIST ECONOMY AND STAGFLATION

In a Proutist economy, stagflation is impossible. In a system where a large portion of stocks and bonds is owned by workers themselves, profits go mainly to workers. A 30 to 70 division of national income between owners of capital and labor is not likely. At the extreme, suppose all income goes to workers; then a $100 deficit in the example given above will produce a full-time job. The deficit will have to be much less than $143 needed in the present conditions.

Let E denote the percentage of excess deficit needed to produce one job in the economy; that is to say, let E indicate the government spending over and above that needed to produce a job in an economy where all property is owned by workers. Then it can easily be seen that

$$E = \frac{S_K}{S_L}$$

where S_K is the share of capital and S_L the share of labor in national income. Here E is the index of income and wealth inequality in the economy. The higher the value of E, the higher is the deficit financing needed to maintain a level of employment close to the full employment level. If, for instance, S_K = ·3 and S_L = ·7, then E =·43, indicating that the budget deficit is higher by 43 percent to produce a job than the case would be in an economy where workers are also the owners of capital.

In a Proutist economy, E is likely to be very small, perhaps as low as ·1. This is because much of the income that now goes to the controllers of industries will then go to workers. Labor income will now equal a certain wage plus its share of the property income. New workers hired will also be paid on this principle.

So far I have assumed that the Proutist economy has the same problem to solve as the capitalist economy. Actually the Proutist system is much more stable than its capitalist counterpart. If there is a fall in the aggregate demand in the capitalist system, the producer fires some workers, who then have to be supported by the government. The government in turn collects money from taxes. Therefore, ultimately the employed taxpayers have to support the unemployed.

In the Proutist economy, workers cannot be fired in the event of a fall in aggregate demand because they all collectively own the corporation. Instead, all workers will have to accept lower wages and profit shares to keep the factories going. In other words, all will have to equally share in the problems caused by low demand, at least until the system either corrects itself or until the government comes to its rescue. There will be no cause for bitterness between the employed and the unemployed. Similarly there will be limited need for the government to manage unemployment compensation programs, thereby eliminating one major cause of Big Government. For if workers are not laid off, the government will not be obligated to alleviate their misery through handouts. The need for Big Government is built into monopoly capitalism. In a Proutist economy, this need is minimal. Hence Proutist policies alone can solve the dilemma of raging stagflation.

In view of the discussion so far in this chapter and chapter 3, the American economy stands in need of the following reforms:

(i) All stocks, bonds and other shares of large corporations producing consumptions goods should be distributed among workers, who will then run factories through their elected representatives. The compensation to current owners of capital should be in accordance with my wealth ceiling formula consistent with the minimum wage. This may mean no more than minimal compensation.

(ii) All industries producing energy and essential raw materials should be socialized and assigned to autonomous bodies for management. The principles of management should be the same as those adopted by businessmen facing keen competition. This reform is necessary to avoid the blackmail of large private corporations producing essential commodities.

(iii) All wages above the income of 80,000 dollars should be frozen. This reform along with (i) would result in the fall of E, the index of inequality, and the need for deficit financing to keep high employment level will decline.[2]

(iv) The inherited wealth should be subjected to the wealth-ceiling commensurate with the minimum wage. This formula has been developed in Chapter 3.

Once the Proutist system takes over, only the

fourth, and final, reform will have to remain in effect. Once society is committed to providing jobs earning at least the minimum necessities, income inequities can never grow out of sight, especially when profits are distributed among workers and the inherited wealth is subject to stiff taxes.

MATERIALISM AND OTHER SOCIAL ILLS

So far in this chapter, I have focussed on the economic problems of American society and argued that they stem chiefly from the social sanction of the unlimited right to private property. The sanctity of this right ultimately derives from the catchy arguments provided by the intellectual acquisiter who has the dominant voice in all affairs, be they economic, social and political. Let us now see how the super-materialism of the ruling class of acquisiters is responsible for other social ills such as drug and alcoholic addiction, high crime, pornography, and so on.

When acquisiters dominate society, slowly and slowly, over generations, the acquisitive mentality filters through the rest of society. People follow their leaders. Therefore if the leaders are acquisiters, all other sections of society gradually turn into acquisiters. When money brings power and prestige, the majority of people also runs after money.

Super-materialism means yearning for material possessions at the expense of subtler pursuits of mind such as activities of art and adventure. The mind of an acquisiter gets divided into thoughts attached to all sorts of materialistic objects. Anything divided becomes weak. Strength lies in unity, not division. Thus excessive materialism weakens the mind: selflessness, by contrast, strengthens the mind by moving it towards its nucleus (also see chapter 2).

134

A weak mind is unable to face external shocks. It falls apart at slight pressure and turns towards drugs and alcohol. Drug and alcoholic addiction then becomes a major problem in an acquisitive society. It is a response of the materialistic mind to find escape from reality.

When materialism filters into the general fabric of life, the crime rate soars. Most of the people want what their wealthy leaders have. They want more money; so do the rich, no matter how rich they already are. But the wealthy control the means of production; they are in a much better position to grow richer than do the poor. They can also, because of their affluence, escape the law for their crimes such as price-fixing and black-marketing. In response, the poor strike back and resort to petty crime. Theft and burglaries become common. But as the concentration of wealth continues, callousness in society grows and the petty crime becomes deadly. Petty thefts lead to violence and murder. The end result is that the materialism of acquisiters eventually gives rise to a horrible rate of crime, which, of course, mainly hurts the weakest sections such as the handicapped and the elderly.

The same gradual process of evolution applies to pornography and prostitution. Because of their affluence, the rich are able to corrupt many gullible and poverty-stricken women. Prostitution spreads, and so does pornography.

The only way to solve all these problems, therefore, is to deny money the dominant role it has in the determination of public policy. This may call for fundamental economic and political reforms, or a revision of the Constitution. But that is the only remedy for all the social ills, for the cure should be directed at the basic cause and not at the symptoms.

If the economic reforms presented above are not introduced, the following is likely to happen in the next two decades.

(i) The rich will grow richer, and the middle class and the poor will grow poorer. The number of the affluent and the poor will rise in the 1980's and then reach alarming proportions in 1990's.

(ii) Crime, prostitution and pornography, already at scandalous levels, will continue to rise.

(iii) Deficit financing will continue, and the government will keep growing bigger, thereby worsening the problem of inflation and unemployment. Eventually a depression would occur, dwarfing the Great Crash of 1929.

(iv) Drug and alcoholic addiction will continue to soar, ultimately reaching into the lives of even children.

The sooner the economic reforms are introduced, the faster will society recover from its illness. True, the reforms call for bold steps; they prescribe a surgical treatment, overhauling the entire system. But when the body social becomes cancerous, surgery is the only cure.

The analysis so far has been conducted in terms of the United States economy and society, but it applies to all Western countries, and for that matter to all nations, for they are all today dominated by the acquisiters. The root cause of problems everywhere in the world is one and the same.

Footnotes

[1]In chapter 3, I had made an assumption that usually nobody becomes rich, by which I mean a millionaire, through an honest living. There might be a few exceptions to this rule, but in prescribing socio-economic policies, one disregards the exceptions and focusses on what is generally valid. Josephson's account of the Robber Barons suggests that many fortunes were made towards the end of the nineteenth century through criminal activities including tax evasion, stock fraud and labor sweating. Some of that money was passed on to their families, which grew richer by means of inherited wealth. Should the extremely wealthy persons of today then be permitted by society to enjoy the fruits of their tainted inheritance? The answer is clearly no, for this allows the perpetuation of gross inequities and violates the principle that everyone should be provided equality of opportunities. Hence there have to be strict limits on inherited wealth in accordance with my formulas established in chapter 3.

Today the Robber Barons have mushroomed. Open any newspaper and you will find rich persons indicted for tax fraud, price gouging, bribery and so on. There are so many oil companies which have been fined by the SEC for cheating customers of billions of dollars. The fines, of course, run into millions, while the price overcharge runs into billions. The laws are weak and riddled with loopholes. On the other hand, the rich defendants can hire smart lawyers and go scot free. The Robber Barons of today are involved in organized crime, drug smuggling, in promoting pornography and prostitution, and in price-fixing in legitimate businesses. They have corrupted society to the core. Even the law-makers—Congressmen, Senators, even a U.S. President and a Vice-President— have in recent years been accused of taking bribery and hush money. They have been accused of using shoddy tactics to keep themselves in power--tactics which one expects only from common criminals.

A petty thief or a burglar, of course, would have been sent to jail if found guilty of the same tactics. But lawmakers have bags full of money, and scarcely do they receive any punishment. That is why, I say, there should be strict controls on the accumulation of wealth. Private property is a meritorious institution. But even the best of things, when allowed to get out of control, recoil on their owners. The wealthy today are running amuck. Society will have to pass laws to eliminate their means of influence.

[2]It may be noted here that in reality E is higher than the number appearing in statistics. This is because the economic muscle of many millionaires enables them to set their own wages in many corporations. What appears as salary in statistics may partly reflect what economists call rent. Hence a part of the high salaries may be attributable to one's control over stocks and bonds. This means that the pay-roll statistics actually underestimate the magnitude of E. Hence freezing top wages at $80,000 per year would in effect lower the value of E.

References

1. Batra, R. N., *The Downfall of Capitalism and Communism: A New Study of History,* Macmillan, London & Humanities Press, Atlantic Highlands, New Jersey, 1978.

CHAPTER 6

PHILOSOPHY OF HISTORY

Sarkar's views regarding society and its or-
ganizations partly derive from his understanding
of history. As with every other subject, his
vision of history is novel and original. Much
like Marx, Toynbee and Spengler, Sarkar detects a
certain pattern in the quagmire of past events,
but his hypothesis, called the law of social
cycle, is more general than similar hypotheses
combined. It is an answer to all the pointed
darts that critics in the past have hurled at once
popular dogmas of historical determinism.

I have examined this subject in great detail
in another book. [1] Here I will present a brief
outline, and let the reader decide for himself how
brilliant and prophetic is Sarkar's diagnosis of
the human past. Sarkar argues that the law of
social cycle has operated without fail in all
civilizations, and will continue to operate in the
future as well.

CHARACTERISTICS OF HUMAN MIND

Every author with a new and deep message to
convey, introduces his own terms, concepts and
definitions. In this respect, Sarkar is no
exception. Even where he borrows a bit from the
stock of already known ideas, especially those of
Marx and Toynbee, his expostion reveals new
insights.

Sarkar's thought is based on a simple and yet
deep perception. It begins with the fact that
society is basically composed of four types of
people, each with a different frame of mind. Some
by nature are warriors, some intellectuals; some
are capitalists and some laborers. This way there
are four broad groups or classes in a community.
Thus Sarkar differs sharply from Marx and other
socialists who define classes on economic grounds
--on the basis of income and wealth. Sarkar, of

course, does not neglect the economic aspect, but to him it is only one of the four aspects describing the totality of society. Class divisions, in his view, exist, and have existed ever since the genesis of Civilization, because of inherent differences in human nature.

The four types of people mentioned above do not, of course cover the full range of society. There are many gradations among the stated groups. Among laborers, for instance, some are highly skilled and some unskilled. Similarly, capitalists did not exist in the past in several societies. In order to provide class definitions independent of time and space, Sarker goes deep into human behavior and commences with the fundamentals -- with characteristics of the mind which he classifies into four distinct categories. That is why every society basically comprises only four types of people which he groups into *Shudras, Khatris, Vipras* and *Vashyas*. To a scholar of Indo-Aryan civilization, these groups relate either to the caste system still lingering in India, or, as in ancient times, to one's occupation. But to Sarkar they convey an altogether different meaning and significance: they simply reflect four types of mind, each manifesting itself in nothing else but one's deeds, thinking, and outlook towards life. Of course, given the freedom of choice, the mental make-up is also reflected in one's occupation. Therefore in the case of society's privileged classes, which are usually free to make such choice, the profession is a true gauge of their mentality.

A Shudra-mind is one that is completely dominated by the environment surrounding it. It is passive, and unintelligent relative to the other types, and those whose actions and behavior exude such mentality are the ones called Shudras. The Shudra-mind fails to do anything subtle or intellectual, for it is ruled by materialistic

thoughts which run parallel to the crude waves of
matter. Sarkar belives that every entity in this
universe emits certain waves and vibrations which
the naked eye cannot perceive. The waves of the
Shudran mind are similar to those of inert matter,
and therefore a Shudra cannot subjugate material
forces or the physical environment in which he or
she resides. Unskilled workers, peasants, serfs
generally belong, or have in the past belonged, to
this class. Exceptions, of course, may be
discerned in all these occupations. Some peasants
or farm workers may be persons of keen intelligence, or there may be other physical workers
who perform hard labor not by choice but under
social oppression. Such persons are not, of
course, Shudras. Similarly, in virtually all
societies in the past slavery was a common institution and slaves were forced to do the servile,
physical work. But in no way does it mean that
the slaves were Shudras. A Shudra is simply one
who performs physical labor either by choice, or
because he or she is unable to acquire technical
skills. Even though imbued with physical
strength, Shudras lack the initiative, ambition
and drive to succeed in the world: seldom do they
shine in society.

The mind that is moved by the spirit of
subduing matter is the Khatrian mind. "To make a
slave of matter," says Sarkar, "is the wont of a
Khatri." [2, p. 14]. Thus, a Khatri is one who
loves adventure, is full of courage and high-
spiritedness, has natural curiosity to learn new
ways, and applies his physical strength and skills
to solve his problems. Since the Khatrian
intellect is subtler (more intelligent) than the
Shudran intellect, the Khatri makes the Shudra do
a considerable amount of his work. The Khatrian
class is usually composed of army officers,
skilled workers, adventurers, professional
athletes, etc.--anyone who struggles to solve
problems through direct fight or physical prowess.

A Vipran mind is one that is more prone to intellectual pursuits than the Khatrian mind. Like the Khatri the Vipra too wants to subjugate matter, he too strives to make the environment conducive to his living, but, unlike the Khatri who wrestles material forces with his heroism and physical skills, the Vipra uses his intellectual forte to attain the comforts of life. The Vipran mind is subtler than the Khatrian mind; hence in social interactions as well as in politics, the Vipra eventually comes to prevail over the Khatri. Thus the ambitious Vipras, lacking in the Khatrian endowments of virility and fearlessness, endeavor to dominate society by controlling the Khatrian mind and through it the Shudra. In Sarkar's words, "The Khatri wants to bring matter under his subjection by a direct fight and the Vipra wants to keep the Khatri, the conqueror of matter, under his own subjection through the battle of wits." [2, p. 36]. Thus, a Khatri's behavior is straight and simple, not difficult to read, but Vipras usually approach a problem in a roundabout way. They devise theories, cults and dogmas to confuse the Khatri and take advantage of his intellectual poverty.

Priests, scribes, poets, scientists, lawyers, physicians, teachers and the like constitute this group. Most intellectuals keep aloof from politics and earn a living by dint of their intellectual caliber; but those seeking high social status and political power attain them by prevailing over the Khatrian mind. Thus, whenever Vipras rule, they rule by winning over the Khatris who alone are physically and mentally equipped to maintain order in society.

Finally, we come to the Vashyan mind. Most people want enjoyment from material things, but the Vashyan mind also has a penchant for their accumulation. In fact, Vashyas, according to Sarkar, "are more partial to possession than to

142

the enjoyment from material objects--want to feel peace in the mind thinking of them or feasting upon them with their eyes." [2, p. 101]. Of the three intervals of time, the Vashyan mind frets constantly about the future and seeks to amass wealth for a rainy day. At some point in time, the affluent Vashya comes to dominate the other three groups by purchasing their services with his opulence. In other words, accumulation of wealth is the lever through which the Vashya seeks not only the comforts of life and the security of future, but also prestige and dominion in sociey. Not all Vashyas, of course, are interested in politics, but those who are usually surge in society by hiring the Vipras. However, before this, Khatris were working for Vipras, and Shudras for the Khatris. So at some point in time all non-Vashyan sections submit to men of fortune--to those abounding in acquisitive mentality.

Let me illustrate the difference in the four mental types through a simple example. If a problem crops up, a Shudra simply ignores it or tries to postpone the solution as long as possible. A Khatri, by contrast, faces it head on, uses his physical prowess, and does not rest until the resolution is in sight. A Vipra applies his intellect, but, if that does not work, either requests help from a Khatri, or attempts to win him over through persuasive arguments. Finally, a Vashya tackles the problem by pouring down his money to hire Vipras, Khatris and Shudras. This illustration does not cover all cases, but pretty much gives an idea of the different attitudes with which men and women in general lead their lives.

Wherever civilization developed, in Africa, Asia, Europe or anywhere else, a careful examination of history reveals this four-pronged division of the social order. Sarkar calls it the "quadri-divisional social system." His categories of mind are broad enough to cover the full range of a mature society. Thus every civilization, which is what we call a mature society, is composed of four sections, each comprising people reflecting the predominance of a certain type of mind. Ordinarily, individual behavior displays two, or even all, of the four attitudes, but, for the most part and especially under duress, only one mentality betrays its true colors. There is a bit of Vashya or acquisitive instinct in each and every one of us, but only a few constantly long for money and make it the summum bonum of life. We are all after a comfortable living standard and social prestige, but some of us attempt to attain them through physical strength and skills, some through intellectual pursuits and excellence, and some by ceaselessly saving money or making more money with money already at hand. In this order, we are Khatris, Vipras and Vashyas. Those of us imbued with little ambition or drive, wanting in basic education and skills of the time are the Shudras.

It is worth noting that Sarkar's division of society into four different groups is very flexible. Social mobility among the groups may occur if an individual's mental characteristics change over time. Through concerted effort or through prolonged contact with others, a person may move into the realm of the other class. For example, a Shudra, under the command of a warrior may become a genuine Khatri, or through vigorous education he or she may become a Vipra, and so on. Similarly the Vipran intellect, through contact with money, may turn into the acquisitive intellect of a Vashya, or a Vashya may turn into a Shudra. Thus even though class distinctions in society, according to Sarkar, derive from differences in human nature, they may or may not be hereditary.

THE THEORY OF SOCIAL CYCLE

Having described the four types of people in
society, I am now in a position to present
Sarkar's theory of social cycle. In accordance
with his quadri-divisional social system, Sarkar
argues that a society evolves over time in terms
of four distinct eras. Sometimes Khatris, sometimes Vipras and sometimes Vashyas dominate the
social and political system. Shudras never hold
the reigns, but at times the ruling class becomes
so self-centered and decadent that for a while
society may have to languish through the disorder
of Shudran times. Thus no single group can exercise social supremacy and power forever. What is
more interesting, as well as intriguing, is that
the movement of society from one epoch to another
follows a clear-cut pattern. Specifically, in the
development of every civilization, ancient or
modern, oriental or occidental,

> the Shudran era is to be followed by
> the Khatrian era, the Khatrian era by
> the Vipran era and the Vipran era by
> the Vashyan era, culminating in a so-
> cial revolution--such a social evolu-
> tion is the infallible Law of Nature.
> [2, p. 40].

This is Sarkar's law of social cycle. Note the
word "evolution." This law of nature is
"infallible," because it is based on evolutionary
principle. Just as human evolution from animal
life is indisputable, just as the onward march of
humanity along the evolutionary ladder cannot be
arrested, so is this movement of social cycle an
inevitable natural phenomenon, whereby social
hegemony shifts from one section of society to
another, from the collectivity of one type of mind
to another. Thus underneath the seemingly hapha-
zard change in society lies the invisible but

145

unmistakable imprint of certain laws of nature:
Social evolution goes hand in hand with human
evolution. It is in such apocalyptic terms that
Sarkar conveys his message. To him society is a
dynamic entity, and perpetual change is its
essence. A civilization emerges with the rise of
warriors, and, after considerable ups and downs,
through the eras of intellectuals, acquisiters,
and physical laborers, it goes back to the warrior
age, only to resume its evolutionary march in tune
with the same old rhythm. This, in short, is
Sarkar's social cycle.

How do we recognize the Shudran era or the era
of laborers? The society of Shudra is one that
suffers from complete lack of guidance, leadership
and authority; one where the so called leaders
become so egocentric that the majority of people,
following in their footsteps, display Shudran
mentality, a mentality ruled by instinctive behavior and pure self-concern. The Shudran era is
then characterized by anarchy, by a lack of social
order. There the family ties are not binding,
people scoff at higher values and finer things of
life, morals are extremely loose, crime is
rampant, and materialsim permeates society to the
core. People of Shudra-like propensities exist at
all places and in all civilizations, but it is
only when society lacks all purpose and the
oppression of the masses by the class of acquisiters is at the maximum that the Shudran era
begins. The state or government may exist in the
Shudran era, but its dominion is not respected.
And in any case the Shudras, despite their majority, do not control the government. The important
point is that the Shudran era arises because of
the self-conceit of the dominant groups who care
nothing for how their actions affect others. For
instance India and many Western countries today
are passing through the Shudran age.

The Khatrian era, or the era of warriors, in

terms of the political and social structure, is
diametrically opposite to the Shudran era where,
as stated above, laborers are in the majority but
the government, if any, is controlled by a
different group of people. In the Khatrian age,
the Khatri-minded persons, though not necessarily
in the majority, dominate society as well as the
government. There the political authority is
extremely centralized in the form of an absolute
government, people are highly disciplined, family
ties are morally binding, social prestige through
physical prowess and feats is earnestly sought,
women are well respected in society and so on.
Vipras and Vashyas enjoy some respect in the
Khatrian era, although they have little say in
governance. But Shudras perform physical labor
for the Khatri, and in the closing stage of this
period, as in that of every other era, they are
mercilessly exploited. However, at the dawn of
the Khatrian era, the ruler respects their contribution and treats them with care and compassion.

The Vipran era is marked by the rise of
priests and intellectuals, though here again the
ruling class does not have to have a numerical
superiority. Many new theories dealing with
various aspects of life are then born.
Intellectuals always rule by controlling warriors
who alone can maintain law and order in the
society. Hence the Vipran age is the age of
indirect rule. Looking back at the annals of
various civilizations, we find that at times
Vipras ruled as priests, and at others as prime
ministers. But in all cases, they ruled in the
name of the apparent ruler, the king, who was
overshadowed by his advisers. This the intellectuals were able to do by confusing the mind of the
warrior with the help of their complex theories.
In order to block independent thinking by others,
the intellectuals devised catchy but illogical
dogmas. One such dogma, popular in all civilizations at one time or another, was, and is, that

147

woman is inherently inferior to man [1. Ch. 2].
As a result, social respect for women went down.
The same thing, for instance, happened recently in
the Vipra-dominated society in Iran.

The Vashyan era bears close resemblance to the
final stages of the Vipran era where Khatris and
Shudras undergo exploitation which is intellectual
in nature. The Vipras, however, are no longer at
the helm of the polity; rather they work for the
affluent class. It is in this era that the practical value of things is reduced literally to
zero. Everything is valued in terms of dollars
and pennies. Human values begin to recede. Art,
music, religion, sports, everything is commercial-
ized. Crime flourishes, family ties again become
loose, and gradually the Vashyan age heads toward
the lawlessness of the Shudran age. At the end of
Vashyan era, all non-Vashyan groups are remor-
selessly exploited by the limitless rapacity of
the Vashyas. Society then passes through a
period, which may be very brief, of the Shudran
age, only to be engulfed in a social revolution,
following which it resumes its march in terms of
another Khatrian era, and so on.

Note that in every age other than the Vashyan
era, the transfer of government may come about
through social evolution or revolution of the
Shudras. This rotation of societal dominance
along the hub of Khatris, Vipra and Vashyas culminating in the Shudran revolution is Sarkar's law
of social cycle. In his view most countries today
are in the moribund phase of the Khatrian age; at
places the Vipran era is about to be established,
whereas in many democratic countries, the Vashyan
or the Shudran period is in vogue.

Examples from Western and Russian Societies

Let us now explore the annals of some well-
known societies and see if they evolved in terms

of the law of social cycle.

Students of Western Civilization generally begin its study with the Greco-Roman era, although some trace it back to the Minoan period and then to the Neolithic age in Europe and the island of Crete. The proponents of the latter view are, however, in minority, for earlier civilizations were strikingly different, and in any case there is not that much known about the ancient European world.

To understand the evolution of Western Civilization, it is indispensable to have some background of the social structure of the Roman Empire, because even though Roman society has long been dead, Roman Law, the Latin literature and some other Latin institutions have survived till this day. At the dawn of the first century A.D., the Khatrian era can be seen to be prevailing in the Roman Empire with Augustus as its Imperator or Emperor enjoying supreme command over the military and the provinces. This is the age of absolutism and the tradition of Roman conquests that had long been established in Rome continues unabated. The chief bequest of the so-called Principate, said to have begun with the ascendancy of Augustus, is the Roman Law which, among other things, affirmed that all humans are by nature equal and have certain fundamental rights that no governments are entitled to transgress.

The system of absolutism reached its zenith in 284 A.D. with the accession of Diocletian. Prior to his reign, the ruler, at least in theory though not in fact, was the agent of the poeple who had some fundamental rights, but now even that semblance of "responsible" government disappeared. The main reason for this change lies in the economic decline of the third century; the people having lost confidence in themselves were ready to forfeit all their rights for the elusive hope of peace and security.

The despotism, however, could only temporarily arrest the downfall of the Roman Empire whose economic and social structure had already been enfeebled by the decline in agriculture, population, commerce and the cities. The lack of a law of succession made the bloody conflicts unavoidable at the time of the ruler's death and the resulting degeneration of the army only accentuated the decay. It was at this time that the Christian religion gained a foothold in society. The Catholic Church succeeded because it provided guidance and shelter to the oppressed at a time when the Roman Empire was crumbling under the wieght of imperialism as well as invading hordes who pounced on the spoils from all directions-- Northern Europe, the Eurasian Steppe, the Arabian Peninsula, the Atlas and the Sahara.

In accordance with Sarkar's law of social cycle, the Church in any case would have inherited power from the decadent Khatrian Roman Empire, but the latter's downfall was considerably hastened by the onslaught of the Barbarian invasions, which led to a lot of bloodshed, pillage and violence. Had it not been for the Church, the Western Civilization would have met its grave at that time; under the spate of invading marauders, the decadent Roman society would have reached extinction, were it not for a little life-breath that vibrated the budding Church. This is how the Vipran era, or the era of intellectuals in the guise of the Catholic Church was born.

At first, of course, Christianity had to struggle against tremendous odds. It is true that older forms of paganism in Rome were losing strength during the first three centuries, but this did not necessarily spell triumph for Christianity. The Imperial Government either suported or tolerated many other cults and religions from

the East. However, with the decline in the social
fibre, Christianity, in spite of tough competition
from other religions, spread quickly, and by the
time of Diocletian's coronation, Christian com-
munities were organized in nearly every city of
the Empire. Even the periodical official persecution of Christians could only slow, but not
stop, the eventual triumph of Christianity over
all other faiths. Most of its early converts were
gained from the slaves and other laboring classes.

In the first three centuries, Christianity
genuinely embodied the teachings of Christ whose
magnetic and selfless life-story dominated the
preachings. This was the main source of strength
in the admirable lives led by the early saints.
With the passage of time, however, especially
after Christianity was recognized as the official
religion of the Empire towards the end of the
fourth century, the Church too succumbed to the
temptations of luxury and bigotry. Having gained
official recognition, the Church no longer
remained the religious society of the poor and the
middle class. In order to acquire wealth and
social adherence, it subordinated religion to
politics and secular affairs. Its bishops and
saints were now interested more in perpetuating
their positions and privileges than in living up
to sublime and lofty ideals. Instead of society
depending on the Church for moral guidance, the
Church became the parasite on society.

During the latter part of the fourth century,
the Church gained ground because the ruler had
been converted to Christianity. This was a marked
reversal from the older days of persecution,
because now the ruler himself encouraged and
abetted the acquisition of opulence and power by
the Church. By the fifth century, the Church had
become the dominant social and even political
power of the Empire. In the name of the Khatrian
king, it was the Church--headed by a Pope, bishops

151

and priests--that ruled society. The Vipran age thus began in the fifth century.

At the behest of the Church, the governmental actions were designed to root out paganism, its rituals and sacrifices, although later on the Church itself felt it necessary to devise rituals and dogmas of its own.

The Vipran age in the West lasted from the middle of the fifth century to about the end of the ninth century. During these four hundred years, priests completely dominated society, with only periodic opposition from the warriors. One such warrior was Emperor Charlemagne who reigned from 768 to 814. During his rule, Charlemagne not only conquered many territories, but he also took control of the Church, thereby temporarily establishing the era of the warriors. Other than that, the Church had few rivals for over four centuries. The priest ruled with the help of his theories which portrayed him as an intermediary between a common man and God. This is precisely how intellectuals rule. Their theories enable them to trap society in the web of complex rules and regulations.

It is during the Vipran age that women lost their high social status that they had enjoyed during the Roman Empire. During the preceding age of the warriors, women had led a very active life. They participated in social, economic and political events. But as soon as the priestly Vipras took over society, woman came to be regarded as inherently evil and a temptress. Man was then supposed to be born to serve God, but woman was supposed to be born to inflate the heart of man. While the Vipras were not sure if woman had a soul, they proclaimed man to be God-Almighty to woman. One effect of all these attitudes was that rape or prostitution became solely the fault of woman [1, C. 5]. And in this respect what happened in Western society, was repeated verbatim in all civilizations.

The Vipran age lasted until the end of the ninth century, when a series of events led to the ascendancy of the Feudal landlords, culminating in European feudalism. The rule of intellect and theories then gave way to the rule of the wealthy. The intellectuals then became subservient to the landlords who possessed the acquisitive mentality or the Vashyan mind. Vipras now justified the dominance of the landed magnates in terms of a new theory called the Christian paternalistic ethic.

The Vashyan age or the era of acquisiters lasted from the start of the tenth century to about the middle of the fourteenth, when some unforseen events, such as the Bubonic plague of 1348, the Hundred Years War between England and France, brought about the Shudran age or the era of conflict between ruling acquisiters and laborers. This was a period of unprecedented crime and near anarchy in Europe. Peasants and lords fought pitched battles, resulting in bloodshed and violence.

The Shudran age, which is usally short-lived, lasted for a hundred years, till about the middle of the fifteenth century when in a matter of 25 years social revolutions broke out in France, Spain and England. In the aftermath of these revolutions, warriors or Khatris came back to power, bringing about another period of absolutism.

The second Khatrian age of the West began around 1460 when Louis XI defeated nobles in France and established a centralized monarchy. In Spain this task was accomplished by Queen Isabela and Prince Ferdinand in 1470's, whereas in England absolutism reemerged in 1485 with the rise of Henry VII who founded the Tudor dynasty. This is how the second social cycle began in the West.

The new Khatrian age lasted till 1689 when a peaceful revolution in England, called the Glorious Revolution, overthrew the reigning king. The Vipras or intellectuals then came to power again, but this time in the guise of the prime minister who, of course, ruled only indirectly--in the name of the new king. During the early seventeenth century, Vipran primacy reappeared in other important areas of Europe as well. In France, following the death of Louis XIV, the kings were extremely feeble, and their imperium was actually enjoyed by their council of ministers. In central Europe, then ruled by the Austrian House of Hapsburg, the role of the prime minister was filled by the State Chancellors who overshadowed their kings and queens.

The new Vipran age lasted till 1860s, when the new Industrial Revolution brought capitalists to the forefront of society. Capitalists, bankers and merchants, who possess acquisitive mentality, then came to prominence. The Vashyas or acquisiters have been ruling the West ever since.

Today the Western society is passing through another Shudran age. That is why there is so much conflict between wealthy corporations and the Shudran labor unions, something reminiscent of the conflict between landlords and peasants during Feudalism; that is why there is so much crime, drug and alcoholic addiction and materialism in society today.

This state of affairs cannot last for long. Social conflict in the West will continue to grow until the wealthy are dethroned around the year 2000. Society will then move into another golden age of the warriors [1, Ch. 9].

This is how the West has evolved. Let us now

see how the Russian society has evolved. A careful analysis of history reveals that Russia was in
the Khatrian or the warrior age from about 800 to
1050, a period known as the early part of Kievan
Russia. Events before the year 800 are not amenable to interpretation because of a total lack of
reliable information.

From the end of the eleventh century to about
the end of the fourteenth, the Russian warriors or
princes were overshadowed by the Russian Church,
indicating the existence of Russia's Vipran age.
Then came the rule of landlords, culminating in
the Russian variety of feudalism. This was
Russia's Vashyan age which lasted from the end of
the fourteenth century to the middle of the
sixteenth. Then came a period of anarchy, or
Russia's Shudran age, which ended in a social
revolution brought by Ivan the Terrible in 1564.
He started another age of absoltism. Ever since
then, Russia has been passing through the new
Khatrian age.

In this respect, the Bolshevik terror in 1917
did not produce a real revolution, for the Russian
society continued under the vestiges of
absolutism. Russia has been in the new Khatrian
age for so long that anytime it could pass into
another Vipran age. And the current conflict between Russian intelligentsia and the State authori-
ties is simply a harbinger of the coming change
where the intellectuals will come back to power.
The intellectuals will bring about the fall of
totalitarian communism and usher in an era of
relative political decentralization in which the
Russian parliament will be supreme. This follows
from an application of the law of social cycle to
Russian society [1, Ch. 8].

So far I have shown the validity of the law of
social cycle in two ancient and diametrically different civilizations. The reader can examine

other societies, and they will all be found to
have evolved in tune with one and the same
pattern. Herein lies the universality of Sarkar's
message. Herein lies its generality and breadth,
its brilliance and vision.

HUMAN EXPLOITATION

If it is necessary to describe the annals of
human past by only one word, then 'exploitation'
describes it better than any other. This
exploitation followed more or less a similar
pattern. Towards the end of each era, the ruling
class would oppress the masses. It would be
opposed by the class next in line of succession,
and when the "opposition" came to power in the new
era, people would experience a temporary relief.
Before long, however, the new ruling class would
become an engine of repression of others, until
yet another class emerged to wrest the reigns of
government, and so on. Thus one class after
another ascended to power in the past in all
civilizations, and exploited the other three in
accordance with its mental characteristics. When
Khatris were at the top, they constantly fought
with each other to expand their empires and in the
process conscripted the Shudras in their armies.
Shudras thus became victims of their ambition.

When Vipras attained prominence, they
inflicted intellectual exploitation on society.
They devised illogical dogmas to bind the Khatris
and through them the Shudras. They started the
oppression of woman, calling her a temptress,
inherently evil, and devoid of soul. They are the
ones responsible for prostitution which began in
the temples. When Vashyas came to power, they
imposed economic repression on the masses. Much
of society's income and wealth became concentrated
in their coffers. Consequently, prostitution and
crime soared during their rule.

The broad pattern of human exploitation just described was repeated verbatim in all civilizations. The question is: can we do something to rupture this age-old pattern? Given that the eternal rhythm of the law of social cycle cannot be broken, is humanity foredoomed to undergo the agony of ups and downs, of momentary benevolence and prolonged persecution? Are we predestined to be trampled, as in the past, under the grinding wheels of oppression perpetrated in turn by three classes of Khatris, Vipras and Vashyas? My answer is a definite no! The law of social cycle indeed cannot be violated, but once we understand the pattern of historical events, we can devise a political system designed to fit into this pattern in such a way that the period of persecution is minimized. What we need is a Constitution that establishes a nucleus of benevolent people who control the movement of the social cycle. Society, like any other entity, is subject to ups and downs. This is the inviolable law of Nature. What we must and can do is to shorten the downward period as much as possible. All this, however, points to a new political system, which is taken up in the next chapter.

References

1. Batra, R. N., *The Downfall of Capitalism and Communism: A New Study of History,* Macmillan Company, London and Humanities Press, Atlantic Highlands, New Jersey, 1978.

2. Sarkar, P. R., *The Human Society, Part II,* Ananda Marga Press, Calcutta, 1967.

3. Toynbee, A. J., *A Study of History, Vol. 1,* Oxford University Press, 1948.

CHAPTER 7

PROUT'S POLITICAL SYSTEM

Every socio-economic system has a political system that supports it. Capitalism, for instance, derives from the social sanction of unlimited private property, of everyone's right to enrich himself no matter how opulent he already is. In such a socio-economic setting, it is not surprising that political power also rests with the class of the rich, the owners of property, who, with the help of mercenary intellectuals, have sanctified capitalistic greed in the unimpeachable garb of liberty, justice and human rights. Capitalism is propped by a political system we call democracy, where at least two political parties compete for people's votes. There are at least two points of view facing the voters. However, none but the rich can afford to seek elections. The candidates, therefore, belong mainly to the class of the affluent. Where then is the choice?

True, the candidates make different promises. They belong to different parties. But their basic philosphy, their life-styles are essentially the same. Hence they all end up promoting interests of one and the same class--the class of the wealthy. Hence spring all the loopholes in the tax system; hence the inconceivable maldistribution of income and wealth in all the so called democratic countries; hence the super-materialism surfeiting society.

Marxism is the other extreme. To capitalism private-property is a sacred word; to Marxism it is an anathma. The social setting in communist countries is that the masses, as opposed to their comrades in power, should enjoy no fruit from property. The State, and its delicate leaders, should have it all. Hence arises the need for totalitarian regimes to choke human freedoms and

159

the natural urge for accumulation. Hence the ugly dictatorships in the name of proletarian welfare.

Thus every socio-economic system rests on the pillars of a congenial political system. Prout is no exception. And as in all other respects, it radically differs from current or past frameworks of government. It is based on strict morality, on what is good and shining in human beings. It contends that ever since the genesis of civilization some six thousand years ago, humanity has been brutally exploited by one class after another. There were, of course, short phases lighted by the ruler's benevolence, but by and large history reveals that the three groups of Khatris, Vipras and Vashyas came to power turn by turn and brutally oppressed the classes not in power as well as the Shudras. Today in many countries Vashyas are at the helm, and for this reason materialism and the attendant malaise pervade the world. (See the previous chapter.)

Is humanity doomed to such exploitation forever? Is there no escape from our inhuman past, or must the past be projected into the future? Prout's answer is in the negative. It contends that although the law of social cycle, being based on social evolution, is inviolable, humanity is by no means condemned forever to the cycles of exploitation. In order to escape from the clutches of the past, those representing the best tendencies of human beings should be established in the nucleus of social order. The staunch moralists and spiritualists should come forward and take charge of the administration of society. For too long the field of government has been left to predatory politicians who can at least temporarily fool the people through sweet words, promises and slogans. Government is a serious matter; the administration of society should not be a play-ground for the self-seeking and the corrupt. It should be in the hands of what Sarkar calls *Sadvipras*.

THE COLLECTIVE BODY OF SADVIPRAS

Plainly speaking, Sadvipras are those persons who cannot even think of acting in self interest. They are honest, intelligent and compassionate persons whose nature is to fight injustice and corruption in society. Since such people represent our best sides, since they are beyond selfishness, political power should be centralized in a board or Collective Body of Sadvipras. From such centralization of power, no one has to fear, because the selfless act only in the interest of others.

One may legitimately ask if such people actually exist in society. For if they do not, the Collective Body proposed by Sarkar is no more than a utopian institution. Sarkar argues that Sadvipras have frequently appeared in the past. Many people gave up their lives fighting the entrenched citadels of corruption; many persons died serving humanity, but, under the pressures exerted by the establishments, society did not take their guidance. Therefore, Sadvipras are indeed rare, but they are there today and will be in the future. Indeed, Sarkar is optimistic that soon society, while reeling under the engines of Vashyan repression, will recognize the services, selfless love and intellectual brilliance of the present day Sadvipras, and then demand that they be placed at the helm.

A Sadvipra has to be a spiritualist. A spiritualist is one who is constantly fighting with his base instincts such as greed, selfishness, egocentricity, bigotry among others. He has no room for illogical dogmas; nor does he tolerate subsisting only for oneself. He is ever prepared to serve the needy, the exploited, and to fight the corrupt, the exploiter. Having realized that the base instincts flourish on mind's attachment for the external world, he turns to the world within himself. He meditates. He makes his extroverted mind introverted, so as to render maximum service to society. For he knows that service to the needy is ultimately the only source of true happiness.

A spiritualist alone can be a Sadvipra. Unlike others, he quotes no books to get his point across, for his knowledge derives from spiritual experience gained from intense meditation and selfless service. Reading books is an intellectual activity. Therefore a person, who has merely read holy books, is an intellectual, not a spiritualist. Everybody, who can read and write, can thus become a religious leader. But to be a spiritualist is no easy affair. Reading books alone will not lead to selflessness. Only intense love for the suffering humanity, combined with dedication, meditation and austerity, will. Dogma breeds intolerance, spirituality universalism. For a broad-minded person, the whole world is his family.

The first mark of a Sadvipra is that he (she) is a spiritualist. The second mark is that he is a great intellectual. Meditation brings intelligence. Hence a spiritualist is also very intelligent. A Sadvipra, therefore, understands the problems of the day. With his intuition he can anticipate incoming troubles. With no selfishness in his heart, he can easily see through the catchy schemes of vested interests. And since he is above all interests, he serves only the masses.

Whenever one talks of a spiritualist, people immediately think of religion or dogma. There can be no greater misconception than this. Religion may or may not be spirituality. A religious person may be fanatic, illogical and self-centered.

But a spiritualist is the complete opposite of that. He has no room for irrational thinking, no respect for those who, for the sake of their God and their own hegemony, impose their dogma on others.

A spiritualist is a scientist. With the help of meditation, he conducts experiments in the laboratory of his mind. He accepts only those subtle truths which he can thus verify.

There are phenomena that the naked eye cannot perceive. A person with a microscope will testify to that. But the spiritualist wants to decipher all mysteries with his naked eye. And his meditation makes his mind so subtle and broad, that he can see what others cannot.

A spiritualist is a fighter. The natural tendency of the mind is to move outwards, to run after external things. Reversing this natural tendency is harder than swimming upstream in a swollen river. The struggle with base instincts of mind is a life and death struggle. Those who do not meditate, but just read books or periodically visit temples for spiritual needs, do not have the faintest idea of how ceaseless and strenuous is the spiritualist's conflict with his mind, with latent obsessions and fears, with innate bigotry and temptations. Only the brave, the mighty can survive and win in this struggle.

The one who has mastered his mind or is striving tirelessly to master it is a Sadvipra. The one who has tamed or is in the process of taming all his infirmities through meditation and self-sacrifice is a Sadvipra. From such a person, no one but the exploiter has anything to fear. But the Sadvipra loves all. He belongs to all. He has kind words even for the exploiter, for he knows that given proper education and guidance, all ruthless hearts can be tamed into selfless

163

ones.

The Sadvipra, however, is not opposed to using force. If someone is earning 2000 times the minimum wage of others because of his selfish hold over property, then the Sadvipra will first request him to give some property to others. He will try to reform him by pointing out the fact that greed is a sickness which ultimately will breed misery for him and others. But the Sadvipra is not going to wait for months before the property owner experiences a change in heart. He is too practical a person to do that. Instead he will incite others to take quick action and take away some property in the interest of social welfare. Hence the Sadvipra combines the qualities of a spiritualist, an intellectual and a pragmatist. He loves everyone, and that is why a Sadvipra alone should be trusted with the administration of society.

Prout argues that political power should be vested with a Collective Body or a board of Sadvipras. From history we know that one class after another came to power in all civilizations. Each class exploited the other three in accordance with its mental characteristics. In the future also, the three classes of Khatris, Vipras and Vashyas will gain prominence in accordance with the law of social cycle. If nothing is done, they will continue to exploit women and Shudras. Therefore, to obliterate all vestiges of exploitation, a Collective Body of Sadvipras, overseeing the actions of the class in prominence, must be established in society. The Constitution should give this body the ultimate power.

The rule of Sadvipras will not be a rule of dogmatic irrationalism and tyranny of the Medieval Age. On the contrary, it will be a rule of logic, scientific outlook and humanitarian love. Sadvipras will make sure that the caprice of the

class in prominence remains under tight leash.
While the Constitution will indeed give them the
final word, their real source of strength will be
their exemplary living and their contact with the
masses.

The role that Prout assigns to this Collective
Body is one of planning and general supervision in
important aspects of life. It does not assign the
Body any legislative, judicial or executive
functions, which are to be performed by elected or
appointed officials in accordance with the
Constitution. Sadvipras, therefore, are in the
nucleus of society. Their major function is to
see that the class in power does not abuse its
authority. Khatris, Vipras and Vashyas will go on
succeeding each other in governing society, but
the repressive phase of their rule will be very
short. Whenever the class in power starts
oppressing the other classes, the Sadvipras will
educate and incite the masses and with their help
enable the succeeding class to come to power.
This way the social cycle will keep on revolving,
but humanity will not have to undergo the upheaval
that it has so often experienced in the past.

Are Sadvipras rare? Yes. But the world was
blessed with them in the past and will be blessed
with them in the future. In any case, Sarkar
shows the way through which any person can become
a Sadvipra. Meditation, selfless service,
dedication, intense love for humanity, and an
indomitable will are the weapons a person needs to
tame the base tendencies of his mind. Any person
who utilizes these weapons and strives for about
twenty years can become a Sadvipra.

To become a Sadvipra is extremely difficult,
but it is not impossible. Once the means are
known, the inaccessible becomes accessible. And
is it not fitting that the leadership of society

should be in those hands which have accomplished what many regard as impossible? Leadership cannot be taken lightly. Responsibility for the well-being of each and everyone rests on shoulders of the one at the helm. Should these shoulders not be rugged? Should they not be battle-tested? One who survives the battle with his mind is the most courageous of all. Is he not our natural leader? Does he not represent our best interests? Is he not our guide in every walk of life? He alone is; not the crooked politician.

There is another reason why people should have no fear from the rule of Sadvipras. Their rise to power will occur only after society gives recognition to their selfless service. Their influence will derive from their contact with the masses and not from any temporal power which will still be vested with legislative and executive bodies. Sadvipras will only have a supervisory role and will be answerable to the general public just as any elected official today is. Society that brought them into power could just as easily throw them out if they were found misusing their positions. Hence there is really nothing to fear from concentrating power in the hands of a group of moralists.

While there is nothing to fear from the establishment of the Collective Body, there is a good deal to be gained from it. Find any country today and you will find massive abuse of power. If there were a Collective Body overlooking the actions of the government, such abuse will not occur. It can be easily seen how such a group at the nucleus would keep the government under leash in a totalitarian regime. But even in democratic countries, where each of the legislative, executive and judicial branches of government are supposed to serve as a check on high-handed actions of the other, the Collective Body would be very useful. In the presence of such a body, the

Emergency would not have occurred in India, or Watergate or Koreagate in the U.S., or the brutal abuse of human rights in Russia, China, Vietnam, Uganda and many other countries. Hence a body of Sadvipras is the need of the day, and the hope of tomorrow. In every country, whether democratic or authoritarian, the ruling bodies are usually composed of people belonging to the same class. Hence they fail to serve properly as checks and balances. Separation of powers is not enough; there has to be another powerful institution guaranteed by the Constitution, an institution whose members stand above all mean and narrow tendencies; which belongs to all classes, and whose word prevails over that of others.

How will the Collective Body of Sadvipras come into being? Here Prout calls for a "selecto-electional" process, that is, for elections of the members of government at regional and federal levels by a large group of voters satisfying certain qualifications. It rejects the idea of universal suffrage, unless, of course, all members of society are honest and highly educated. The idea of 'one person, one vote' sounds sweet and appealing, but it never works that way in practice. Rich politicians have usually been able to buy votes from some people not only in India but in many advanced democratic nations. This is simply a mockery of the election process, and the fault here lies not just with the affluence of the politician but also with the poverty, illiteracy and irresponsibility of those voters who are thus sold out to money. If the election process is to be above board, then only those with integrity and education should have the right to vote. Hence Prout advocates the formation of an Electoral College whose members satisfy the following qualities: They should

(i) be educated to the extent that they understand the pros and cons of proposals made by

167

those contesting elections,

(ii) have a sense of responsibility and a socio-economic consciousness,

(iii) and, above all, be honest.

Prout preaches that every person should be provided the opportunities to imbibe such qualities, but until that is achieved the membership of its Electoral College will have to be restricted to ensure true and impartial elections. "Without a proper system of selection," says Acharya Raghunath, a close student of Sarkar, "democracy gets degenerated into 'mobocracy,' thereby creating a circumstance of exploitation." If all the voters possessed civic consciousness then politicians will not be able to get elected by appealing to regional, parochial, racial and caste sentiments.   Big business and money will have little role to play in the election process, and only then will democracy have a chance of success.

Prout does not reject the idea of democracy, only the current system of elections that in reality produces an oligarchy of the affluent. For democracy is 'rule by the people, for the people, of the people,' but the present-day election process reduces it to 'rule by the rich, for the rich, of the rich.' And the rich then exploit the general public in the name of public welfare. They offer a little bonus here, a little carrot there, while pocketing millions in their vaults. Hence to ensure democracy, to ensure that the interests of the poor and the masses are not neglected, political power has to be centralized in the hands of those who feel for the poor, the downtrodden, the handicapped.   Not those who merely say that they feel for the poor, nor those who mask their ugly actions by making eloquent speeches, but those who have demonstrated through their actions the capacity to suffer for others. In the hands of such Sadvipras alone can the people repose their trust. Thus what Prout in effect suggests is that the essence of democracy can be preserved only if the current system of controlled elections by the opulent gives way to one of a powerful Collective Body of Sadvipras elected by an Electoral College with membership ultimately running into millions.

In order to expand the scope of this Electoral College, Prout suggests that institutions should be established to provide moral and social education to people, thereby qualifying them as voters. Such institutions should be free from any political influence; they should be administered by an independent body like the Election Commission or the Public Service Commission, and their curriculum should be carefully designed by experts--educationists, sociologists, philanthropists, spiritualists among others.

Those who pass the tests of such institutions should alone be the members of the Electoral College which may be divided into regions or administrative units to elect candidates for various arms of the government. The candidates themselves will, of course, have to come from the Electoral College, that is, they too will have to satisfy certain qualifications of education and integrity.

The Electoral College should not only elect members of various legislative and executive bodies, but also the constituents of the Collective Body vested with the supreme authority. The process of election by the selected voters should be direct. Even though the Collective Body is given ultimate authority in the land, with no other body restraining it, there is no possibility of autocracy or totalitarianism for various reasons. First, the Collective Body provides collective leadership, and power is not vested

with one person only. Secondly, it is answerable
to the mass-conscious Electoral College and ultimately to the general public. Thirdly, the members of the Collective Body themselves satisfy
certain credentials of honesty and integrity.
They can never go against the common good and
welfare. Finally, the Proutist system calls for a
full guarantee of all human rights including the
right to free speech, criticism, assembly and
employment. As long as the media are free and
independent, no system is likely to lapse into
autocracy.

In the Proutist system the role of the
Electoral College is not over even after it has
elected members of various political bodies
including the Collective Body. It will continue
to remain in touch with the people and apprise
them of the points and counter-points of various
socio-economic issues. Constant vigil is required
to make sure that all the arms of government function efficiently and honestly, and this vigil will
have to be exercised not only by the Collective
Body but by the ever watchful Electoral College as
well.

In present democratic systems, government's
actions and policies are carefully examined by
opposition parties and the press. This is a
healthy practice which serves to keep the official
caprice under control. But it also has its
faults. Quite often the opposition engages in
destructive criticism, or plays upon the narrow
tendencies of the public. The party in power
counters with the same game, and, as a result, the
country does get two viewpoints of any issue but
not necessarily the best viewpoint. The Electoral
College that Prout calls for will have a different
role to play. Since it will not belong to any
faction or party, it will be able to offer
constructive criticism of government's policies.

WORLD FEDERATION

Prout belives in universalism and hence in one world government. The entire universe is our joint property; therefore every person has the right to settle anywhere in the world. Restrictions imposed by various nations in the free inter-country migration of people are reflective of narrow tendencies of the mind. In most cases they manifest nationalism, but in some they reveal racism and bigotry. All these restrictions conflict with the spirit of universalism, and hence are eventually doomed to extinction. For only that which is cosmopolitan eventually survives and then endures for ever. This has been the trend in every civilization in the past as public loyalty has gradually expanded from villages to towns to provinces and now to nations. The next broad-minded step is not internationalism, but universalism. This is because internationalism simply calls for cooperation among various nations without destroying the virus of nationalism. In any case, this concept is already tainted, because it has been so blatantly abused by the communist giant, Russia, which has furthered petty national interests in the name of Marxian internationalism.

Prout advocates universalism, and for this calls for the spread of a common ideology based on spirituality. It professes that we are all children of the same cosmic parents, (cosmic consciousness) and nature (the operative principle), and the universe is our common abode. All other philosophies and dogmas which collide with this sentiment of cosmic inheritance are devisive, and hence the cause of all the friction. Humanity is the same everywhere, and only this sentiment can unite humankind and eventually lay the foundation of one world government.

As regards the structure of the world

171

government, Prout favors the formation of a world federation with two legislative chambers--a lower council and an upper council. The lower council should consist of representatives elected by each country on the basis of its population, whereas the upper council should be composed of a fixed number of representatives from each country. In this arrangement, all countries, even those with small populations, will find due representation. All legislation should proceed from the lower council, but it cannnot be passed without the approval of the upper council.

At the outset this world federation may act only as a lawmaking institution, whereas the administration of various regions may continue to be vested in the local government of each country. As a result, says Sarkar, "it will not be an easy affair for any government to oppress the linguistic, religious or political minorities according to the whims of the governing majority."[1, p. 31.]. Various countries have various laws for various crimes. The very idea of crime and virtue differs from country to coutnry. Prout realizes that one world fraternity is impossible as long as different definitions and laws regarding crime prevail in nations. Justice cannot and ought not vary from country to country. Hence among the first tasks of the world federation will be the bridging of the gap among criminal laws of various countries. In general, virtue consists of all those actions that further human development in mental, physical and spiritual spheres, whereas vice comprises those activities that hinder social development in these three spheres.

The formation of world government also necessitates the acceptance of one common language. English should now be accepted as the international language without inhibiting the development of other languages at the country

level.   However, conditions may vary over time,
and languages are also subject to death.
Therefore in any period, only that language which
is in maximum use in different parts of the world
should be accepted as the world language.

The basic rules guiding the world federation
are the same as those guiding the national
governments. The five fundamental principles of
Prout as well as its economic program apply to
the world government as well.   Thus, it will be
the responsibility of the world federation to provide minimum physical requirements to all human
beings, and so on. Maintenance of law and order,
and the vital raw materials such as oil, coal
among others should be vested with the federation.
Similarly, there should be a Collective Body of
Sadvipras for the whole world.

References

1. Sarkar, P. R., *"Problem of the Day,"* Ananda Marge Puclications, 854 Pearl Street, Denver, Colorado, 1959.

CHAPTER 8

PROUT: AN EVALUATION

In the preceding chapters I have introduced the reader to the fundamental principles of Prout and the economic and political reforms that flow from them. It is now time for an evaluation, for a panoramic view of where Sarkar's system stands in relation to other schools of thought.

That Prout differs from any socio-economic system prevalent in the world today or in the past is amply clear even from a cursory reading. But is it a serious system--serious enough to warrant study, intellectual debate and criticism? Is it simply a hotch-potch of religion and secular philosophies or a rational ideology with a well thought out basis rooted in human needs and psychology? Many people, especially in India, have heard of Prout, but few have studied it, and fewer still have understood it. Many others have submerged its message under the barrage of official propaganda and denunciation.

This is extremely unfortunate, because in my view Prout has indeed many new ideas to offer. All systems in the world today are cracking under the weight of ultra-selfish materialistic philosophies. Capitalism is tottering; communism is artificially propped by authoritarian machines; and the underdeveloped countries are torn by poverty, corruption and internal conflicts while some rich but dictatorial oil producing nations bilk them of millions year after year. The world has exceedingly grown interdependent. Can any country today prosper without international trade and cooperation? Can anything happen at a place today without creating ripples in other parts of the world? The need of the hour is a common ideology and universalism offered by Prout.

Prout is the first comprehensive theory which comes to grips with the requirements of economic development and one world government. This state

ment will perhaps startle many economists and
social scientists who have worked in the fields of
economic development and internationalism. But my
stress is on the word 'comprehensive.' True, many
ideas that Prout offers have been offered before.
And in this respect I differ with many of Sarkar's
students who regard Prout as a completely original
philosophy. Some of its ideas have in fact been
expounded by others before--Bertrand Russell,
Toynbee, Tawney are conspicuous examples--but
Sarkar is the first one to realize the unity between spiritual and material needs, between spiritual and secular ideas. He is the first one to
offer a philosophy which is comprehensive, logical
and intensely practical.

Eonomists have written thousands of papers
regarding a country's economic growth; they have
provided myriad theories as to what should be done
to improve living standards in underdeveloped
nations, but the underdeveloped nations continue
to be as poor as they were before these theories
came into prominence. This is because these
theories are not comprehensive. They treat the
symptoms of the problem of poverty without
diagnosing the underlying malady. Some suggest
that the poor nations should follow the path of
capitalistic development, while others exalt the
virtues of Marxist command economies. The underdeveloped countries have followed both these
paths, but their problems of poverty are as
staggering as they were three decades ago. Today
many economists call for increased foreign aid,
while others insist on increased foreign trade.
All these ideas are one-sided, and that is why
developmental experiments of so many nations have
ended in a fiasco.

Sarkar sees virtue in all these ideas, but
even if their best is combined together, they will
not be enough to generate economic and social
development. If the path of private ownership

176

and capitalistic growth is followed, many under-developed countries will perhaps eventually prosper, but it will take them two or three hundred years. For this is precisely the time that developed nations such as England, France and America have taken to be where they are today: They did not grow rich overnight. Furthermore, despite fabulous growth, these nations have passed through internal catastrophes and turmoil. Today they suffer from air pollution, drug addiction, pornography and prostitution, abominable crime rate, a horrid divorce rate and other social tumours that do not afflict underdeveloped nations to the same degree. Do the underdeveloped nations want to repeat their mistakes, commit their follies? Above all, do they have hundreds of years to come up to where the developed nations are today? Of course not! Nor do they have the capacity to inflict the kind of horror that Stalin let loose on his hapless citizens so as to promote rapid industrialization, nor the capacity to undergo the purges that China inflicted on its moot denizens during the Cultural Revolution.

The whole world, including the underdeveloped countries, today faces two alternatives in its forward movement--the path of monopoly capitalism or of State capitalism (communism). Sarkar propo-ses a third alternative: economic development based on the foundation of morality. To the de-veloped world, Prout offers social and spiritual progress through its program of rational distribu-tion and the establishment of the Collective Body of Sadvipras. It offers them a reprieve from eco-nomic uncertainty and mental tortures of material-ism. To the underdeveloped world, Prout offers rapid economic development unaccompanied by the modern ills of capitalism and Marxism. Private ownership has been tried, and so has been the State ownership. Both have failed the poor countries. The path of morality is yet to be tried, and this will not fail.

The model of capitalist development says that the state should lend all encouragement to owners of capital in establishing factories, hiring factors and determining the wage rate. Capitalists will then save more money, increase their investments, hire more workers, and all this will contribute to a rise in total wages, profits and national income. With no State intervention, producers will reinvest a considerable part of their profits, and so on, so that year after year the national economy will grow at a healthy rate. The distribution of income will, of course, become more unequal, but that is a small price to pay for rapid increases in employment and national income. The proponents of capitalism, however, forget that capitalist economies are subject to shocks of recessions and depressions, that extreme income inequities foster social ills afflicting the capitalist world today, and that small-firm capitalism eventually turns into monopoly capitalism which leads to grossly inefficient use of material resources.

The Marxist model of development, on the other hand, vests the ownership of all land and factories in the hands of the State, which now does the task of saving and investing, and of wage and price determination. This model calls for the abolition of private property, and since it collides with the natural human urge for accumulation, it has to become repressive and authoritarian. It must continue to trample all the fundamental human rights for its existence, as can be seen in Russia, China and other Marxist countries today. Besides this repression, the communist system is patently inefficient because the State planers are themselves corrupt, and also because it destroys the human incentive to work hard.

The underdeveloped countries, as stated before, have followed one of these two models, or a combination of them, and it is no wonder that they continue to languish in the abyss of poverty.

Prout establishes a connection between morality and economic development. Human greed provides powerful stimulus for growth, and finds its full-blooded expression in capitalism; the State power can also brutally goad a person to work hard, save more or consume less, and has found its culmination in the Marxist mode of development. But transcending these two forces that propel us to work hard is the force of self-sacrifice. Towering above greed and the state command is human conscience which can inspire a person to perform miracles. Many people in the past accepted torture rather than a compromise with principles. The authoritarian commands could not bend them; nor could the lures of money. They were great moralists. They were humans like you and I, but they had in them a spark that would not bow to the weapons and wiles of tyranny. Hence morality transcends brute force and human avarice, and it is this force which Prout intends to harness to achieve rapid economic development. The connection between morality and economic growth is thus very real, for consuming less and saving more can be presented before the people as an ideal which will lead to physical, intellectual, and spiritual development of the entire society.

At the practical level also, it can be easily seen that without moralistic government, economic development can be a long-drawn-out-process. Billions of rupees in India have been invested in the economy in the course of its five year plans, but a considerable portion has gone into the coffers of ministers and petty bureaucrats. Is this, may I ask, economic development, or a diabolic joke of those professing to serve the people? Is this economic or personal development? Hence springs Sarkar's call for morality; hence his stress on the need for a Collective Body of

179

Sadvipras who will give effect to a just, efficient and honest plan for economic prosperity.

I started my evaluation of Prout by suggesting that it is the first comprehensive theory of economic development. Its 'comprehensiveness' lies in the fact that it sees the need for reforms not only in economic spheres but also in the social, educational and political spheres. For a nation's economic health depends not only on efficient functioning of its economy, but also on its social and political structure supporting that economy. The economy may be streamlined, its industries may be overhauled, but if its political structure is corrupt, real progress is impossible. Therefore, Prout argues that the political and educational reforms must precede any thrust for economic development.

Prout is an eclectic philosophy. It sifts the best out of various theories, blends them with morality and spirituality, and then produces a magnificent flower with so many ideas defly arranged as its petals. Marxian humanism finds expression in Prout's emphasis on a guaranteed minimum living standard to all, a 'minimum' that includes food, housing, clothing, education, and medicine, that varies from place to place, and that must be made to grow over time so that the gap between the minimum and the maximum real wage rate is progressively reduced. Prout, however, rejects the Marxian ideal of complete equality, but adopts Rawls' sense of justice and humanism. Rawls has argued that "all social values--liberty and opportunity, income and wealth, and the bases of self respect--are to be distributed equally unless an unequal distribution of any, or all, of these values is to everyone's advantage" [7]. Compare this with Sarkar who writes, "Except when a special favor becomes necessary to give certain individuals impetus and inspiration, all persons must be given equal rights and opportunities in all spheres" [8]. Basically, therefore, it is Rawls'idea that finds expression in Prout's system of rational distribution which accepts inequality of income so that the economic incentive given to socially more productive persons will enable society to raise welfare of the worst off section of the population. Furthermore, the rational distribution formula presented in Chapter 2 is also practical and capable of managment without recourse to official repression. For the abolition of private property and hence of inequality, being in violation of natural human instincts, can be accomplished only in an autocratic framework.

Until now my appraisal of Prout has been at the philosophical level. Let me now closely examine the theoretical basis underlying its economic program. I have already analyzed Prout's idea of rational distribution and found that it is a superb blending of egalitarianism, economic incentives and a sense of justice. Let us now explore Prout's program of industrialization.

First of all, Prout accepts the highly popular view that industrialization is essential for economic development, but, by according agriculture the status of an industry, it does not slight the role of agriculture. It thus favors Nurkse's idea of balanced growth in which the State has a definite role to play, but in which the private initiative is to be encouraged and channeled into small scale industries where it becomes an engine of social progress rather than an engine of social evil.

Prout's economy does not derive from any one theoretical idea; it puts together a number of practical ideas commensurate with its own broad version of individual and social welfare. Thus, while it calls for State ownership of some key industries producing raw materials on a large scale, it also favors large and small scale industries independent of State control but managed by representatives of workers. Most of the essential final commodities that make up the minimum wage basket are to be produced by cooperative firms, whereas some luxury goods may be produced by private owners on a small scale. There are thus two basic ideas underlying Prout's economic framework: the theory of economic decentralization, and the putting-out system.

The virtues of economic decentralization in a monopolistic system are well known. If large scale industries are managed by workers themselves, there will be profits but they will mostly be distributed among the workers, thereby avoiding the ill effects of extremely skewed income distribution. In addition, these firms will be more efficient, because workers will work harder and have little incentive to go on strike. Much of labor unrest and friction will thus disappear. The cooperative firms will also be more amenable to mechanization which will not result in lay-offs but in diminished working hours. Actually this will only occur in the short run. In the long run, the firm introducing new machinery may be able to expand output to such an extent that the working hours need not be reduced. If anything, the employment opportunities might even expand owing to overall economic growth.

In any case, the system of cooperative firms is much preferable to the capitalistic firm where the producer fires workers at the slightest economic shock, leading to bitterness and economic uncertainty for those who really toil for society. Under capitalism, where workers often resist technical change for fear of being laid off, several working hours are lost because of countless strikes. On top of this, there is so much monopoly induced waste and inefficiency.

The concept of economic decentralization also

manifests itself in the separation of producing raw materials and final commodities. Many giant multinational firms today unfairly restrict competition by controlling their sources of raw materials. Economics call it vertical integration, a situation where a firm producing final goods also produces its own raw materials. This invariably leads to increased concentration in an industry and to many other abuses directly responsible for inflation. Prout, in effect advocates what is sometimes called vertical disintegration, where the production of raw materials is separated from the production of final goods.

The other idea underlying the Proutist economy is reminiscent of the putting-out system which was the primary form of manufacturing organization in western Europe from the early sixteenth century to the mid-nineteenth. Although its remnants are discernible in places today, since the second-half of the nineteenth century, the putting-out system has gradually given way to the more integrated form of economic organization--the factory or the firm. The most important characteristic of the putting-out system, as pointed out in Chapter 3, is a merchant middleman, a putter-out. Prior to the rise of factories, this middleman supplied raw materials to skilled and unskilled workers who mostly worked in their homes. At times, he supplied them with machinery also, but the important point is that work on the machines was generally not carried out under one roof. Later, the middleman recovered the goods from the workers and either took them directly to the market or to another batch of artisans for a second stage of manufacturing. The system perhaps originated with Italian textiles but later it spread to many other industries such as mining, iron, furniture, paper, ship-building, pottery among many others.

The most relevant feature of this system today is that it resulted in economic expansion through industrialization in many rural areas which loom large in most, if not all, underdeveloped countries. If this system is even partially adopted, the rural sector can be industrialized without transporting rural labor to towns and cities, thereby avoiding all the material and psychological costs associated with such transformation. Sarkar's example of how the cotton textile industry should be organized resembles this historical system, except that he favors the State to be producing raw materials on a large scale basis, thereby reaping all the benefits of mechanization, and then supply these raw materials and machines to rural and urban workers who could produce finished goods at home. The scale of production of the final goods could vary from industry to industry. There is no need to supply obsolete machinery to workers, who could thus be highly productive while working at home or a place nearby. These workers in turn could supply their goods to consumers'cooperatives which will market the finished goods.

Sarkar's program of industrialization therefore is a modified version of the historical putting-out system. It combines the efficiency of modern methods of production with the old economic organization which is suitable to the economies of underdeveloped countries today. I have called it the pyramidical system of production, because, in this, key industries constitute a big base on which large and small scale industries are to be built as various steps of a pyramid. Each higher step rests on the one below it; the whole arrangement requires keen coordination. This, one might say, is Prout's version of balanced growth, wherein agriculture, being one of the industries, is a step on the economic pyramid.

This modified version of the putting-out system is an excellent idea which, I believe, holds the key to economic growth of the poor

184

nations. Most of them suffer from high unemployment, low capital stock and inadequate levels of
industry. Industrialization is necessary for
their survival, but this goal conflicts with the
need to rapidly generate employment opportunities
on a massive scale. However, the pyramidical economic system will industrialize the rural areas
without drastically disrupting the rural life;
simultaneously it will create the necessary
employment opportunities. It will also require
less capital stock to produce a given level of
output, for some goods that are now produced in
large buildings could be produced in homes. As a
consequence, the economy's requirement of overhead
capital will go down: the result will be a fall
in overall capital-output ratio and hence a rise
in the rate of growth.

The pyramidical economic system, which draws
inspiration from the twins of economic decentralization and the putting-out system, has many other
advantages absent in the capitalistic frame.
Industrialization, either under monopoly or under
State capitalism, has given rise to large scale
pollution and destruction of the environment. The
reason lies in the fact that the economic de-
cision-makers themselves do not have to suffer
from the side effect of this so-called progress.
Under monopoly capitalism, producers are bent on
profit maximization and they care nothing for how
their factories pollute the air or contaminate the
rivers. In the State-capitalistic systems, the
condition is just as bad, if not worse. For the
central planner, while sitting in cozy buildings
far removed from the scene of action, has little
idea of how his policies affect the environment.
He has to fill certain production quotas, and no
one worries about the side effects. Above all,
industrialization in both capitalist and communist
countries has produced workers' alienation as the
production process has become more and more imper-
sonal.

In the pyramidial system, however, workers are to be involed, as much as possible, in the production and decision-making process. The entire industrial set-up is to be humanized, so as to reduce this alienation. Furthermore, if workers manage the industries, then being producers as well as consumers, they are likely to make sure that their factories do not harm the environment in which they live. For instance, if a new technique is to be introduced, they would try to minimize its side effect, i.e., introduce pollution controlling devices as well. This is a far cry from the current economic systems where the centralized economic power has blindly incorporated mechanization with little regard for the subtler aspects of life, including a healthy environment.

PROUT AND NIEO

Let me now turn to an idea which is currently popular with scholars specializing in international economics: the new international economic order (NIEO). The idea has been floating around for more than two decades, but since 1973 when OPEC succeeded in quadrupling the oil price, it has received a remarkable impetus and attention. The message of those calling for NIEO, in a nutshell, is that the current international trade and monetary system is at least partly responsible for the poverty in underdeveloped countries, and that the developed countries must among other things

(i) increase their foreign aid to developing nations,

(ii) provide them with general debt releif,

(iii) index the prices of goods exported by developing nations with goods they import, and

(iv) lower their trade barriers which inhibit exports from developing countries without demanding any reciprocal trade relief.

These demands are certainly compatible with the universalism preached by Prout which advocates the distribution and utilization of world's resources in such a way that every person is provided with the minimum standard of living and that the gap between the minimum and the maximum real wage rate is progressively reduced. But from the Proutist viewpoint the NIEO is destined to failure for various reasons. Firstly, given the pervasiveness of extreme materialism in economically developed countries, it is too much to expect them to transfer anything more than a neglible amount of resources to the poor nations. But even if by some stroke of miracle, they agree to a substantial level of foreign aid, the corrupt officials in developing nations themselves will squander away all this aid just as they have done in the past. True, some affluent persons will grow more affluent than before, but real economic progress will not occur. Economic development in the poor nations not only requires international economic reforms, but reforms in domestic economies of the developing countries as well. It requires not only a new international economic order, but also a new international political order. But above all, it requires a shift from the current materialistic ideology in all nations to a humanitarian basis of life.

The demand for NIEO by some intellectuals may be compared to India's Bhudan movement which was started by Vinoba Bhave in the 1950s, and which has miserably failed. If the poor have to rely on the rich man's change of heart for an improvement in their economic conditions, then they will have to wait forever. Any theory based on this idea is impractical. The Bhudan movement was one such idea which sought to persuade the big landlords in

India to transfer a portion of their lands to the landless laborers. Sarkar had written about the intellectual bankruptcy of this movement as far back as 1959, when it was still popular among Indian intellectuals. Today this idea has been all but discarded, but it might have delayed the passage of laws requiring mandatory land reforms, which, of course, have still not been implemented.

What about Prout--is it a practical idea? In the present world milieu, I find practicality in all of Sarkar's views except his call for the Collective Body of Sadvipras. The socio-economic reforms flowing from Prout are needed all over the world which suffers from tremendous inequities existing not only within but among all nations. The minimum and the maximum wages must be interrelated everywhere so that all humans at least meet their minimum requirements. Similarly, in all nations stocks and bonds of private corporations producing consumption ·goods ought to be distributed among workers so that income inequalities never grow out of sight.

These are some of the ideas that can be materialized in the world today. But the body of Sadvipras is another matter. In a world where mutual distrust prevails among races, religions, philosophies and nations, is it possible to identify a group of Sadvipras who appear to be super-human beings? Ours is the age of materialism; can this age be the cradle of completely selfless sages? Ture, such sages did appear in the past, and will in the future; but they were rare. Should we expect them to appear in a cluster today or at some future date?

Sarkar seems to realize that the present world ideology and environment are not fertile for the rise of Sadvipras. Perhaps that is why he takes recourse to futurism, suggesting that Sadvipras will most certainly come to power in the future;

rather, people will demand that Sadvipras be given the supreme authority to put an end to the wretched living conditions generated by those entrenched in the seat of power.

Sarkar's optimism is not without foundation. For he has prescribed the path by following which anyone can become a Sadvipra. Meditation, dedication, intense love for the suffering humanity, austerity and tireless struggle with one's mind are the weapons that one needs to become a selfless being. This is a formidable arsenal of spirituality, one known to us since ancient times. This is the arsenal for salvation. But Sarkar prescribes the use of this arsenal not only for personal salvation but also for the salvation of society. And the beauty of it all is that there is not an iota of narrowness and irrationality in his message. It is universal, although from a distance it may appear unreal. It is only a matter of time that by utilizing the variegated weaponery of morality provided by Sarkar, some people will become Sadvipras.

There is no doubt that Prout's comprehensive economic program is superior to NIEO. For the success of NIEO is at best dubious, whereas that of Prout is assured. True, Prout requires revolutionary changes in thought all over the world, but if it is revolution that is needed, then it is revolution that should be preached, not some theroies which are basically faulty and only deflect attention from multifaceted reforms.

PROUT, OPEC AND MULTINATIONAL CORPORATIONS

If two tumours afflicting the world today are to be singled out for their virulence, then the Organization of Petroleum Exporting Countries (OPEC) and the multinational corporation (MNC) are way out in front. These tumours are fast becoming cancerous, if they have not already become so.

Both derive from single human disease--greed.   If the world body is to survive, both have to be tightly controlled.

The rise of OPEC is recent, but the MNC has existed for a long time.   It may not be unfair to say that OPEC was infected by the virus of its predecessor.   For until 1973, the multinational oil companies exploited the petroleum producing nations to the hilt, as they offered them only one dollar and eighty cents for a barrel of oil.   The oil companies were vertically integrated.   They produced their own crude, refined it and marketed it through their own gasoline stations.   They had the monopoly and the monopsony power, with the result that the OPEC, which was formed in 1960, had to beg for every small rise in oil's price. Of course, the oil companies reaped hefty profits which mainly benefited their own executives.

The situation took a drastic turn in October 1973 during the Egyptian-Israeli war when Saudi Arabia, out of political considerations, imposed an oil embargo over the world; and soon, to the amazement of all including the OPEC, the oil prices shot up, as the oil importing nations scrambled for tight supplies.   The OPEC nations awoke to a new reality, namely that as a cartel they could do what the multinational oil companies had done all along; that they could extort huge proftis from the rest of the world by curtailing their production and jacking up their price.   They increased the oil price manifold and have been continually doing so ever since.   Today the oil price has gone up by 2000 percent over its pre-embargo level.

Is there any justification for OPEC's actions? Could we call it a case of reverse-justice where the once hapless OPEC nations now take revenge against the MNCs involved in oil?   Not really. For the profits of the oil companies are higher

190

than ever before. Under monopoly capitalism using
administered prices, profits usually go up with
the rise in raw material costs; and the oil companies are among the worst oligopolies. The OPEC
is indeed taking a sweet revenge against its
former exploiters.

While the OPEC and oil companies profit as
never before, the rest of the world has to pay a
heavy ransom. Steep rises in oil prices have
definitely pinched the Western world, but they
have proved catastrophic for the underdeveloped
countries. It is the poorest nations that have
been hurt the most; while their debt has
sky-rocketed, the OPEC greed shows no signs of
abatement. OPEC is running amuck like a drunk
bull and it bludgeons the rich and the poor alike.

The oil cartel provides a classic justification for Sarkar's insistence that the production
of vital raw materials such as oil should be
completely under the control of a central
authority, such as the world federation. No private company or nation or group should be permitted to be in a position to blackmail society.
Only a world government can assure this. For the
good of the world, the OPEC has to be controlled.

Given the divisions in the world today,
prospects for such control are gloomy. Oil prices
will continue to rise through one pretext after
another. For this is the nature of the rich. No
matter how much physical wealth they have, they
want more. From my calculations, oil production
will drastically fall in 1985-86 owing to political considerations. As a result, first Europe and
then the rest of the world will be plunged into
the worst depression ever. The OPEC might disappear in the aftermath.

THE MULTINATIONAL CORPORATION

While OPEC has turned predatory only recently, the MNC has been plundering the poorer sections of the world for a long time. The plunder began during the colonial times when the MNCs from Europe spread their tentacles over the colonies. They invested in plantations and raw materials, paid lowly wages and inflicted dismal terms of trade over the servile nations. All this, of course, subsidized the standard of living in rich countries.

Since the second world war, the home of the dominant MNCs has shifted from Europe to the United States. The MNC today is not only a menace for America, it is a menace for the whole world. For the assets of the MNCs are rising much faster than the assets of local or "national" firms. As a result, as with the U.S. and European economies, the economy of the whole world will become oligopolistic with all the attending ills. Today the distribution of income and wealth within the U.S., Europe and other nations is extremely skewed. Soon, with further spread of the MNCs, it will get worse. The rich will grow richer and the poor grow poorer all over the world. The social ills of Western society will also then come to afflict other countries. Crime, drug and alcoholic addiction, family disharmony, social indiscipline etc., are all the by-products of excessive materialism of the acquisiters, the class now in prominence in the West. When the MNCs export their technology to other countries, they also export envy and their greed. The social ills of the West will eventually infect many other nations.

While the MNCs do more harm than good to most countries, their impact on the underdeveloped economies is, and has been, disastrous. Aside from their exploitation of the colonies in the past, the profit making goals of the MNC are in direct conflict with developmental goals of the poor nations.

The MNCs have aroused a great storm of controversy not only among the politicans but also among intellectuals. There are those who plead for the global corporation by pointing towards its record of unprecedented growth; they applaud it for being an efficient engine transmitting advanced technology all over the world. Many other, however, assail its penchant for profit maximization that brings it into collision with needs and aspirations of the host countries. Much of this debate among scholars has been at the empirical level, and its theoretical aspects have been neglected. As a result, the proponents of the MNC have at times implied that their opponents do not really have a grasp over economic theory.

I myself have been exploring the controversy afresh. In two papers, Hadar and myself [4] and Ramachandran and myself [3] have constructed theoretical models examining the decision-making of the MNCs in developed European economies. Among others doing this are Horst [5], and Itgaki [6]. The consensus emerging from these studies is that (i) the MNCs have increased economic interdependence of the developed economies, (ii) their economic impact in general has been favorable, and (iii) any minor problems they have caused can be corrected through an appropriate set of tariffs and taxes on international investment.

In another paper [2], using the same mathematical tools commonly employed in the pure theory of international trade, I have shown that, as far as the underdeveloped countires are concerned, MNCs cause (i) unemployment, (ii) national income loss and (iii) foreign exchnage shortage by inflicting unfavorable terms of trade through the mechanism of transfer pricing. In arriving at these conclusions I have made the same assumptions regarding production functions and technology that are commonly made in trade theory. But while my mathematical model is new, the economic explanation of my results is old. In the case of developed countries, the MNCs have usually taken their capital and technology to some specific industries and then set up their own plants and factories or purchased outright the local firms in host countries. The developed host nations have thus benefited not only from the transmission of more efficient technology and managerial know-how, but also from the inflow of capital. Since the political situation in developed countries is relatively stable, investments are not considered inordinately risky and a relatively small portion of excess profits is repatriated to the country of origin, i.e., the source country.

In underdeveloped countries, by contrast, the investment by the multinational firms has been paltry in comparison to the vast degree of economic control that they exercise. In other words, the underdeveloped world has been the recipient of superior, though profusely capital-intensive technology, but not of much foreign capital. Citing Fajnzylber, Richard Barnett and Ronald Muller report that during 1957-65 the multinational firms of U.S. origin financed 83% of their investment in Latin America from local sources—either through reinvested earnings or from local banks. Thus, less than one-fifth of total investment of the U.S. firms in Latin America during this period was an inflow of foreign capital.

This practice—which perhaps is attributable to uncertain political situation in many developing countries-has the effect of either generating or accentuating severe imperfections in local capital markets. For one thing, the local banks and businessmen are only too eager to lend money to the credit-worthy giants, and this creates scarcity of capital to the local firms which already suffer its pinch. Secondly, the high credit rating of the multinational firms enables them to borrow money at lower interest rates than those that the local firms have to pay, thereby causing a capital market imperfection. Such imperfections may also be caused by the host nation's courtship of the multinational capital. Thirdly, as the local firms face paucity of capital, they become easy prey for outright acquisition. Barnett and Muller report that during 1958-67, 45 percent of all manufacturing operations by the U.S. based firms in Latin America involved takeovers of domestic industries [1].

As regards employment opportunities, apologists of the multinational firms allude to the thousands of workers that these firms employ in less developed countries; however, the concommitant shortage of capital to indigenous firms produces loss of employment there, and the net effect on employment is ambiguous. The U.N. statistics, however, show that the unemployment situation in the underdeveloped countries where the multinational firms operate has actually deteriorated. Finally, the multinational firms have usually thwarted the efficacy of any income tax policy by the host countries by manipulating transfer prices on export transactions, i.e., by lowering the prices on goods exported by a subsidiary to the parent firm. On the whole then, the activities of multinational corporations have proved detrimental to the economic health of underdeveloped countries, although part of the blame, I think, rests with the faulty policies of the host countries themselves.

How can the MNCs be controlled? As I argued in chapter 3, before these mutinational giants, even sovereign democratic governments shudder. What chance then do the poor underdeveloped nations have? Prout does suggest some practical measures in this regard, but only keen coordination between the United States, the home-base of most of the powerful MNCs, and the rest of the non-communist world can exterminate the global evils of the global enterprise. The Proutist reforms that I have earlier suggested for a nation can be reformulated for the world economy. They are given as follows:

(i) All firms producing vital raw materials should be nationalized everywhere in the world, and their operations should be assigned to autonomous bodies responsible to national governments and ultimately to the world federation.

(ii) The OPEC nations should also be made to give up control over their oil concerns.

(iii) The stocks and bonds of all other giant firms, including the multinationals, should be distributed among their workers. The evil, let me point out here, is not the bigness of the firms, but the greed of the multimillionaires who spread materialism because of their aura of success. The MNCs could be a boon to society if they did not constantly hanker after profits, if they only invested their money in rural areas of underdeveloped countries to generate more housing, to fight pollution, to provide clean water to millions. But, for such humanitarian projects the multinationals display no concern.

The Proutist reforms suggested above are the only ways through which the twin evils of the OPEC and the MNCs can be controlled. Other half-hearted measures such as NIEO are mere palliatives destined to meet the fate of India's Bhudan movement. It must be remembered that any institution based solely on human greed eventually brings about ruin. The sooner it is controlled, the better it is. Otherwise, when it dies its own death, it takes others with it.

The trouble with scholars today is that they continue to think in narrow nationalistic terms while humanity's problems have acquired international dimensions. Both capitalism and Marxism are in practice ultra-nationalist systems. Only the cosmopolitan spirit of Prout can cure socioeconomic ills pestering humanity throughout the world.

The good and welfare of everybody in the world, the rich, the poor, the handicapped, the capitalist, the communist, the socialist, the religious, the atheist, of all, lies in implementation of the fundamental principles of Prout. Prout is universal. It is not a reaction to the present-day malaise in the world. It seeks to harness all three aspects of human personality-the physical, mental and spiritual. Because of its universality, Prout will materialize one day. But our full-fledged support to it will hasten the demise of corrupt establishments and the dawn of the benevolent age which will mark an unprecedented break from thousands of years of past human suffering and exploitation.

References

1. Barnett, R. J. and Muller, R. E., *Global Reach: The Power of the Multinational Corporations,* Simon and Schuster, New York, 1974.

2. Batra, R. N., "Multinational Corporations and Economic Development," presented at the conference on the new perspective of India-United States economic cooperation, August, 1979.

3. ‑‑‑‑‑‑‑‑and R. Ramachandran, "Multinational Firms and the Theory of International Trade and Investment," *American Economic Review,* June 1980.

4. ‑‑‑‑‑‑‑‑and J. Hadar, "The Theory of the Multinational Firms: Fixed and Flexible Exchange Rates," Oxford Economic Papers, 1979.

5. Horst, T., "The Theory of the Multinational Firm: Optimal Behavior Under Different Tariff and Tax Rates," *Journal of Political Economy,* 1979.

6. Itagaki, T., "Theory of the Multianational Firm," *International Economic Review* 1979.

7. Rawls, J., *A Theory of Justice,* Harvard University Press, Cambridge, Mass., 1971.

8. Sarkar, P. R., *Ananda Sutram,* Ananda Marga Publications, 854 Pearl Street, Denver, Colorado, 1967.

CHAPTER 9

SARKAR'S VISION OF SOCIETY

In the foregoing pages, I have examined Sarkar's contribution to history, economics and political science. To Sarkar, these apparently diverse subjects are interconnected. We cannot analyze one without analyzing the others. All this enables me to present an integrated account of Sarkar's vision of a human being and society.

"Human existence," says Sarkar, "is an ideological flow." That is to say, every person has a certain mode of thinking, a certain ideology which may be materialistic, intellectual, spiritual or a combination of the three. The ideological flow may vary with time, but all our actions at any moment reflect a certain line of thought. For the sake of all-round progress and harmony in life, we need to focus on all three aspects of our personality--physical, mental and spiritual. If only the physical aspect is exalted, we become extremely materialistic; society may then develop economically, but spiritual and moral values lag behind, and as a result pornography, drug and alcoholic addiction, family problems, crime, social conflicts and indiscipline eventually soar high enough to make everyone's life miserable. This has been the path followed by Western democratic and communist countries. They have advanced materially, but are now confronting insurmountable social problems despite unprecedented prosperity.

If we focus excessively on intellectual development and disregard the physical and the spiritual, we are bound to develop ill health, arrogance and eventually bigotry or mean mentality. A person may then become an intellectual giant possessing vast knowledge, eloquence and pedantry, but his resulting arrogance invariably hinders his spiritual development and hence mental happiness. Similarly, a society which emphasizes the mental aspect to the exclusion of the other two eventually grows sickly and intolerent of other people's views. That is why all societies that were once dominated by priests, who exalted dogmas at the expense of true spirituality, bred intolerance and wars of religion.

Finally, if we attend mostly to our spiritual needs, that is, meditate hard or pray a lot, and neglect the physical aspect of our existence, we will lack the desired harmony, and even the spiritual progress will be slowed. Similarly, if the society focuses primarily on the spiritual, or on dogma and rituals in the name of spirituality, it will painfully lag behind in the economic sphere; this will ultimately impede its spiritual advance as well. For subsistence comes first, and then do subtler aspects of life. This has been the case with India, China and some other eastern societies, and today they are finding it difficult to ensure even a minimal living standard to their people. True, they have a rich spiritual heritage, but all that fades into insignificance if they cannot properly feed their citizens.

The upshot is that for a smooth overall progress, each person as well as his society have to attend to all three aspects of life, otherwise tensions will emerge and some people will be exploited by others economically as well as intellectually. This, in short, is Sarkar's message; this is his vision of a human being and of human society. All his writings manifest this central theme. The goal of our life, to him, should be the merger with the supreme infinite consciousness, but we should move towards this goal through meditation, physical exercises (yogic asanas and sports), intellectual pursuits--including true education, sciences, arts--and above all social service. All this should be done because they are all in our own interest. By following this track and by serving others, we ultimately serve ourselves. This, and this alone, leads to mental happiness.

But if certain individuals move along this path, and society does not, then only a few will develop while the large majority undergoes untold sufferings. Welfare of some individuals will be maximized, but not of all. Hence the entire society has to be so organized as to further human development in all three aspects of life. All its institutions--economic, artistic, social, politi- cal--have to be geared towards this common end. None can be overlooked, none can be separated from others. If economic reforms are introduced, but the political structure remains decadent, all efforts towards general prosperity will prove abortive. Similarly, if political institutions are overhauled with no change in others, no lasting good will result. Therefore, when Sarkar advocates economic reforms, he combines them with reforms in political institutions as well. When he speaks of the world federation, he speaks of the need to spread a universal ideology as well, for otherwise, the world government will remain only a visionary's dream.

Sarkar's is a unique and sublime vision of society. There is no aspect of life that he does not touch. All his views derive from his singular concern for individual and social progress in all spheres. His ideals rise to dizzying heights, and he has faith in the ultimate nobility of every human being. His Sadvipras, as I have said before, are superhuman beings. If we can recognize them, then we should have no hesitation in putting our trust completely in their hands. They alone should have the supreme authority to shape our destinies in all three spheres, not corrupt politicians whose actions contradict their eloquence, nor any dictators who suppress all our human rights and liberties.

PROUT: THE ALTERNATIVE TO CAPITALISM AND MARXISM

Sarkar's manifold contributions are all original and unorthodox. They challenge the stereotyped thinking; they humble the parochial views by their cosmic spirit and universalism. And it is no wonder that they have met fierce oppostition from all quarters in India; it is no wonder that they have been misunderstood, intentionally misinterpreted and abused. This is a misfortune for which the Indian society so far has paid a heavy price.

Sarkar is not only an intellectual giant but also a great spiritual teacher and a social worker. To give vent to his ideals, he has started a socio-spiritual organization called Ananda Marga, which currently has centers in major cities in over seventy countries. Prout may then be regarded as the philosophical base underlying the socio-economic program of this organization.

INDEX

Absolutism, 114, 147, 149, 153, 155

Acquisitive mentality, 114, 134, 144, 154

Acquisitive society, 135

Administered prices, 191

Agriculture, 46, 62-64, 80, 87, 90, 94, 150, 181; and pollution, 74

Allocation of resources, 32, 51, 66-73; and capitalistic greed, 68; and State greed, 76, 77

America, 52, 85, 177 (also see the United States)

Ananda Marga, 204

Atiriktam, 30, 31

Atom, 5, 6

Augustus, 149

Australia, 56

Balance among physical, mental and spiritual activities, 23, 24

Balanced Growth, 90, 181,184

Balassa, B., 58, 95

Barnett, R. J., 195, 198

Batra, R. N., 26, 95, 138, 158, 198

Bertrand, T., 58, 95

Bhave, Vinoba, 187

Big Government, 2, 127, 133

Bolshevik revolution, 155

Bombay, 78

Bulgaria, 58

Captial goods, 69-71

Capitalism, 3, 53-56, 58, 66-69, 73-75, 99, 113-138, 159, 175, 177-179, 182, 185, 197

Capitalists, 52, 139, 140, 154, 178, 197

Carnegie, A., 120

Centralization/Centralized authority, 114, 147,161

Centralization of economic power, 64, 185

Ceiling: on wages, 35, 40; on wealth, 1, 40-44, 60-110

Charlemagne, 152

China, 20, 46, 69, 78, 177, 178, 200

Christianity, 150, 161

Church, 150-152, 155

Club of Rome, 80, 81

Collective body, 22, 23; of Sadvipras, 161-73, 177, 179, 188

Commoner, Barry, 79-81, 85, 95

Communism, 3, 66, 68, 69, 99, 100, 155, 175, 177 (see also Marxism)

Consumer sovreignty, 67, 72, 73

Constitution, 157, 164, 165, 167

Cooperative farming, 64

Cooperative firms, 1, 46-49, 52, 56-58, 61, 71, 72, 93, 182

Corporate serfdom, 53, 54

About the Author

Dr. Raveendra (Ravi) Batra is Professor of Economics at Southern Methodist Univeristy, Dallas, Texas, U.S.A., having previously taught at Hindu College, Delhi, Southern Illinois University and the University of Western Ontario. He is the author of *Studies in the Pure Theory of International trade, The Pure Theory of International Trade Under Uncertainty,* and *The Downfall of Capitalism and Communism: A New Study of History.* He has also authored numerous articles on world economic problems in learned journals. An article in *Economic Inquiry,* October 1978, ranks him as one of the top five economist "superstars" in universities in North America. For 1980-81, he is a Visiting Professor at Vanderbilt University, Nashville, Tennessee.